YOUR
newborn .
promise
PROJECT

A CHRISTIAN PRE-PARENTING PRIMER FOR HUSBAND & WIFE

YOUR
newborn
promise
PROJECT

A CHRISTIAN PRE-PARENTING PRIMER FOR HUSBAND & WIFE

CALLIE GRANT, AUDRA HANEY, AND CHARISSA KOLAR

Graham Blanchard

Austin, Texas

Your Newborn Promise Project
A Christian Pre-Parenting Primer for Husband & Wife

http://www.grahamblanchard.com

Library of Congress Cataloging-in-Publication Data in Progress

Cover Design & Illustrations: Missi Jay

Interior Book Design: Suzanne Lawing

The "Newborn Facts of Life" are adapted from *Spiritual Parenting in the First Five Years: God's Plan for Early Childhood Christian Discipleship* by Callie Grant.

Scripture quotations are from NIV: THE HOLY BIBLE, NEW INTERNATIONAL VERSION®, NIV® Copyright © 1973, 1978, 1984, 2011 by Biblica, Inc.® Used by permission. All rights reserved worldwide.

Scripture noted ESV: The ESV® Bible (The Holy Bible, English Standard Version®). ESV® Permanent Text Edition® (2016). Copyright © 2001 by Crossway, a publishing ministry of Good News Publishers. The ESV® text has been reproduced in cooperation with and by permission of Good News Publishers. All rights reserved.

Scripture noted KJSV: Scripture taken from the New King James Version®. Copyright © 1982 by Thomas Nelson. Used by permission. All rights reserved.

Printed in the United States of America

1 2 3 4 5 6 7 8 9 10

Dedication

Rob, Jack, and Zachary Kolar
Cory, Norah, and Lydia Haney
Michael and Anna Michelle Grant

Because of you we are growing into the
wives and mothers God planned for us to be.
We are grateful for your love and support and
all the joy you bring in our walk with Jesus together.

—CK, AH, CG

newborn promise
YOUR
PROJECT

Question 95

Newborn fact of life
What questioning can do in marriage & family
   1. Grapple with God
   2. Recognize the enemy
   3. Tether to truth
Plan ahead

Persevere 125

Newborn fact of life
What persevering can do in marriage & family
   1. Stay safe in the fold
   2. Lean on the faithful
   3. Keep it simple
Plan ahead

Now What? 155

Notes 159

From the Authors 164

Acknowledgements

We gratefully acknowledge the many people from all walks of life who have inspired, encouraged, and committed hours to supporting the Newborn Promise Project and its mission to serve expecting and new parents.

Many thanks to our home churches, and their leaders and staff for pastoral and theological guidance, including Brad Thomas, Brian Wallace, Phillip Williams, Tracy Hearnsberger, and Amy Taylor at Austin Ridge Bible Church of Austin, TX; Matt Warner and Naomie Bragado at Cornerstone Fellowship, Danville, CA campus; and Northstar Church of Knoxville, TN.

Many thanks to our video team, Jamie and Nathan Jennings and Craig Cunningham for their enthusiasm, determination, and creativity, and also to Mark and Debra Smith and Rick and Susan Pohle.

Graham Blanchard's outstanding panel of Mom Mentors has given support in spirit and with editorial input including Tiffany Malloy, Jill Williams, Kona Brown, Susan Heim, Julie Kieras, and Chere Williams.

Much appreciation also to Amy Ezell, a wife and mother who is passionate for the Lord, and for expecting and new parents. Her steady encouragement and affirmation has spurred our work along from the very beginning.

None of this would be possible without the Newborn Promise team and supporters graciously assembled by our Father. Missi Jay, Rusty Shelton, Katie Schnack, Shelby Sledge, Lynda Greene, Ansley Kynes, Suzanne Lawing, Cory Haney, Rob Kolar, and Michael Grant were instrumental in making it a beautiful new reality.

We love you all.

Your Purpose and Potential

It is significant that God's first recorded interactions with husband and wife took place in a garden (Genesis 2-3). Unlike the dense, sprawling wilderness he created, the garden reflected his deliberate, skilled cultivation of nature for beauty and enjoyment's sake, for resting in the cool of the evening together with him.

God's creation serves as a vivid classroom for his ways. Gardens require interactivity, cooperation between God, who provides the seeds and nourishes them, and his gardeners, who tend and cultivate them.

Adam and Eve were given open range within the lovely dwelling place, but one thing God commanded they must not do: consume fruit from the tree of the knowledge of good and evil, or else they would die. Satan came to plant doubt about their good-willed Father. But they did not need much more enticement. They took the fruit and ate it, terrible seeds, flesh, and all, bringing the wages of disobedience on themselves, on creation, and on every generation after them.

Even before God expelled Adam and Eve from the garden, they expelled him from their hearts. This rejection of God's good will was a rejection of his love and intimacy with him. The human story for thousands of years has been the long slog of regaining that Paradise lost.

Pouring yourself into a study like *Your Newborn Promise Project* and reaping the benefits of drawing closer to God, you will realize the great tragedy of the Fall. As described in Hosea and elsewhere in the Old Testament, God likens his people's break with him to adultery—the devastation not only of a physical bond, but above all a spiritual one.

When the time was just right, God sent his Son to rescue and reconcile humanity on the very personal, individual level (Romans 5). Jesus never mentioned the Fall in his ministry but addressed the conditions it created and announced the remedy: "I am the way, the truth, and the life" (John 14:6). Those who believed in Jesus would start on a new path, born of the Spirit. This gift, God's grace, is the good news of Jesus, his Gospel:

"How can someone be born when they are old?" Nicodemus asked. "Surely they cannot enter a second time into their mother's womb to be born!"

Jesus answered, "Very truly I tell you, no one can enter the kingdom of God unless they are born of water and the Spirit. Flesh gives birth to flesh, but the Spirit gives birth to spirit" (John 3:4-6).

The life, death, and rebirth cycle of a garden beautifully illustrates the spiritual potential a new phase in life holds for you and your family. The arrival of a child can be a watershed event for husband and wife. God brings your newborn into the world already primed to know and to grow in him. As you become parents, you also enter a new phase in your marriage and personal development.

Beautifully—supernaturally—God offers this confluence of transitions to bring you all closer to him. The Newborn Promise Project is designed to spiritually assess and plan for this exciting new season, to permit God to heal and transform you in the most beneficial way, and to be firmly established in a life-saving faith (1 Peter 5:10).

Your newborn promise project is to spiritually assess and plan for this watershed season.

God's Word and the experiences of believers throughout the ages will be our guides, as we exercise our fundamental spiritual abilities to *love, remember, seek, question,* and *persevere.* We will explore how the Bible urges these actions, again and again, for our everlasting benefit. Following three marriage and parenting applications of these abilities, you'll use them in related exercises to Learn, Absorb, Praise, and Connect (Psalm 86:11-13). God uses these pathways for spiritual formation and development in children and parents alike:

Learn – Growing in knowledge of God and your purpose with him.

Absorb – Assimilating facts of God into your heart and meeting with him there.

Praise – Remembering God in everything you do with gratitude and reverence.

Connect – Strengthening ties within your family and community to grow love.

Spiritual life with God is remarkably logical and cohesive, just like the rest of his creation. And so we introduce each chapter with a Newborn Fact of Life for you to prepare for the intertwining of your faith with your child's to form a bond not easily broken (Ecclesiastes 4:12, John 17:21). Our prayer is that you embrace God's personal plan for you in the challenging and miraculous days ahead.

Love

Because we are created in God's image, love creates a spiritual bond, not a physical one. Marriages and families are primarily spiritual unions of love. The Bible depicts love best. Let's look closely at what God says about love.

Newborn Fact of Life

Your child is made in God's image for love.
You will help grow it.

God pours eternity into developing hearts. He plants seeds of long-ing and love for him as life takes shape in the hidden place. Before we even see the light of day, God knows us through and through. Spiritual life begins in earnest with life itself (Ecclesiastes 3:11, Psalm 139).

As God plants in the heart, he also scatters his boundless mira-cles throughout creation and time to draw us near (Romans 1:20). Once born and growing, children can believe in God as easily as they breathe. They come in his image to a world made especially for them.

He casts the starry night with fireflies dancing to the hum of cica-das. Only God could do that! He made the consoling puppy licks that bring a smile and soothe a scraped knee. He abides in the uncondi-tional arms that cuddle on Grandma's porch swing. Jesus loves me, *this I know.*

Sharing such miracles of life with a child is one of parenting's greatest pleasures. All of the adult ho-hum familiarity with this world falls away when the first elusive bubble escapes a giggling grasp—an unguarded, precious moment gathered up into eternity like so many more to come.

Magical moments like these in early childhood help us experience God's love in subtle and grand gestures all around. And with hearts already primed to know him, loving God in return can be as natural as the awe inspired by a rainbow. We were made to love him.

Saint Thérèse of Lisieux related her experience caring for two young girls, the oldest being six. "It was a real delight to see how they believed all I told them," she recalls in *The Story of a Soul*. "Those innocent souls were like soft wax on which any imprint could be stamped—of evil, alas, as well as good," she writes. "Many, many souls would become most holy if they had been properly guided from the very start."[1]

What is proper guidance for young souls in the reality we live in today? How do parents help children grow in their natural affinity for God, and how do parents keep from being the cause of any alienation from him?

The truth is, only God can draw a child to him (John 6:44, Ephesians 1). He does so, generally, through his miraculous creation, and personally, through special revelation and his Word. As such, parents need only to join

> "Many, many souls would become most holy if they had been properly guided from the very start."
>
> —Saint Thérèse

in what God has already started. But he charges us to join in intentionally, prayerfully, and with all the wits and wisdom that only God can give.

The job of fostering a child's love for God and others takes more forethought, insight, and practice, than any other aspect of parenting. We have to trust that when we fail, and we will, that God will help us make amends. Our hearts will be quickened and wrenched along the way. Mistakes will be made. They are part of our learning and growing. God will make us into gardeners and shape our souls while we tend so thoughtfully to our child's.

"I know God needs no help to carry out his work of sanctification," Saint Thérèse concludes. "He lets a skilled gardener rear rare and delicate plants. He has given him the necessary knowledge, but he fertilizes them himself. That is exactly how he wishes to be helped in cultivating souls."[2]

In nurturing your child's rare and delicate soul, consider the task not one of making a good person, but one of encouraging a soul who loves God. Outward acts of obedience and service will naturally flow from that kind of love, one guided by the faith of a child.

What Loving Can Do in Marriage & Family

Place me like a seal over your heart,
like a seal on your arm;
for love is as strong as death,
its jealousy unyielding as the grave.
It burns like blazing fire,
like a mighty flame.
Many waters cannot quench love;
rivers cannot sweep it away.

—Song of Songs 8:6-7

Romantic relationships are so widely depicted in art, literature, music, and movies, that it's hard to imagine not being influenced by them. They show us the many ways people fall in love, express love, make love, argue about or embrace love, and then manage to have a happy ending.

"I am always in hope of making a discovery there," painter Vincent Van Gogh wrote in a letter, "to express the love of two lovers by a marriage of two complementary colors, their mingling and their opposition, the mysterious vibration of kindred tones."[3] As beautiful as his art and words are, Van Gogh never achieved his goal.

In fact, love eludes any artist's attempt to give it full justice, to convey the mysterious bond that it forges and that drives humankind in all worthy pursuits. That is because love creates a spiritual bond, not a physical one. Marriage is fundamentally a spiritual union, dominated largely by the unseen world. And so the spiritual health of the marriage determines the love of the growing family.

The greatest masterwork to ever depict this kind of love, along with the beauty and the mess that humanity makes of it, is the Holy Bible. It's fair to say that the most widely quoted words about love are found in it. The description of love that Paul gives in 1 Corinthians 13 brings to mind admirable qualities of a person you would like to meet or marry. This love "always protects, always trusts, always hopes, always perseveres. Love never fails." We all want to know this love.

The passage resonates so much with Christians and non-Christians alike that portions of it are often recited at weddings and worked into vows—because we really want the words to be true of the person we marry. Then, like so many other good intentions declared at new beginnings, the pledge of ardor tends to fade into pretty words without much force in the trenches of daily family life. Wouldn't we like that to be different?

The possibility is there. Because Paul's words describe God's perfect love, which he freely offers to us. With God, Jesus said, all things are possible (Mark 10:27). Such love can be lived out, in the fullness of its promise, with God's trustworthy help. But we must start with *God* as our love's aim.

It's important from the beginning to step back, gaze up, and mentally embrace God's love as our starting point in marriage and family. Each of us, as individuals, need to be reminded of who we are because of God's love. With this intake of grace, we can more truly reflect in our home *who* we are and *how* we are. We operate from an abundance rather than a dry well. Then, growing spiritually as individuals and as a married couple in the reality of God's love, we will naturally embrace spiritual parenting for our child.

To give our family this solid foundation, we must look closely at what God says about love. The most important command the Lord gave his chosen people was to love him. Jesus said, "Love the Lord your God with all your heart and with all your soul and with all your mind. This is the first and greatest commandment" (Matthew 22:37-38). Then he taught what that means: how to love him, all the benefits of doing it, and the consequences of not doing it. Jesus affirmed this greatest commandment, and he demonstrated the lengths to which God's own love will go.

Never before—and never since—in all of literature or lore has a god commanded such love from his creatures, much less created them for that very experience. And never has a god of any other religion demonstrated what love looks like, nor promised immediate and eternal rewards for this voluntary act.

This great God of love did not create humankind because he was lonely but because he loves (Genesis 1:26, Jeremiah 31:3, John 1:1-4, Acts 17:24-28, among many others). In his very Being—Father, Son, Holy Spirit—God's unlimited love pours forth, and his desire is for his creation to respond and exude it, to enjoy this love that is better than life itself (Psalm 63:3).

In God's creation, all roads in life must be charted by and lead to love. God's gift of love is the answer for every evil and ill. Are you having trouble in your marriage? The answer is love. Do your in-laws drive you crazy? The answer is love. Are you overwhelmed at times by your circumstances? The answer is bittersweet love.

God's love is the power that endures and prevails. It sustains creation, bringing up the sun each day on a miraculous planet filled with an infinite variety of life. It reaches down to an inner place we didn't know we had and exerts its own strength in our being (Ephesians 3:16-18). With overwhelming evidence, Love, in reality, never fails.

Even as love is a blazing fire wielding a mighty flame, it is an endless spring that revives the soul and douses life's deadly foes. Here are just a few everyday ways love can exert its power within you:

Love douses pride. Of all the propensities humans have, pride is the least attractive and the most spiritually dangerous. We all have a fair measure of pride, even as we dislike being around people who display it. "The proud hate pride—in others," Benjamin Franklin observed.[4] Today's hierarchical workplace is ripe for posturing for position and hoarding authority. But in our most intimate relationships we must especially resist pride.

Pride fuels revenge. It takes credit where credit isn't due. Pride leads to power struggles and war—in the home and among nations. Pride ignores the God who made an unfathomable universe and humbled himself as a servant to it. Pride demands to be served.

Love, on the other hand, "does not envy, it does not boast, it is not proud. It does not dishonor others, it is not self-seeking, it is not easily angered, it keeps no record of wrongs" (1 Corinthians 13:4-5). When we feel a swell of pride, whether it nurses a bruised ego or a sense of superiority, our antidote for the poison is love. Let even a slight recognition of your own pride be a nudge for you to pivot toward love instead. You will notice an immediate difference.

Love douses selfishness. In work, play, and relationships, there is a fine line between selfishness and self-preservation. Let's face it: We live in a "me first" world. If you don't look out for yourself, who will, right?

But as we grow in love, self*less*ness grows with it. Love helps us develop a new economy. The inner dialog might go like this: "Oh, you want to sleep in tomorrow? I really want to sleep in. But I want you to feel rested. Okay, you can sleep in, and I'll wake up with the baby." Over time, the jockeying to take care of our own needs becomes unnecessary because the members of a family are looking out for each other first.

Love douses indifference. We are bombarded with things to wring our hands over. If we were emotionally involved in all the issues we read or hear about, we would probably lose our minds. Immediate family life has enough problems of its own. Often a first line of defense against conflict around us is to wall off our heart.

But by responding to the world's and our family's problems with love rather than a seeming indifference, we fuel our life-giving reservoirs of hope and faith. God's love reinforces our heart, and gives us firm confidence to protect, hope, trust, and persevere. We can refuel with God's love every time we pray. Praying for others allies us with God in his even greater love and purpose for them. Praying is caring—loving—in action, and it begets more love.

Applying It in Marriage and Family Life

You already have committed to love and the lasting ties of marriage. Now we will exercise three biblical perspectives on loving that will be highly beneficial for your role as a spouse and new parent. In the following sections, you will:

- **Examine the human anatomy**. Get a clear window on the human make-up, the unseen parts that make you *you* and that serve as the seat of love.

- **Set your heart on devotion**. Expect your love to grow into a soul-pleasing intimacy within your family and with God.

- **Know love's greatest strength**. In this world we certainly all have trouble. Embrace the path of Jesus to overcome and transcend it.

1. Examine the human anatomy

One of the teachers of the law came and heard them debating. Noticing that Jesus had given them a good answer, he asked him, "Of all the commandments, which is the most important?"

"The most important one," answered Jesus, "is this: 'Hear, O Israel: The Lord our God, the Lord is one. Love the Lord your God with all your heart and with all your soul and with all your mind and with all your strength.' The second is this: 'Love your neighbor as yourself.' There is no commandment greater than these."

—MARK 12:28-31

Loving God wholly with all my heart, mind, strength, and soul—my whole being—is the basis of my faith and is foundational for loving my spouse and raising our new child.

Some of the first words children learn are *eyes*, *ears*, *mouth*, and *nose*. They learn more details about human anatomy as early as elementary school, studying the parts of the body and what they do. Today, a mom and dad can even see how their baby's parts develop in utero over the course of a pregnancy. It's an amazing, humbling sight!

Yet for all the scientific advances, formal education, and prenatal planning, the fundamental fact of human make-up goes largely ignored: We are primarily spiritual beings, ruled by our unseen, non-physical lives. What's more, we live in a predominantly spiritual world ruled by unseen forces (Ephesians 6:12). Something else is at work, as any child knows by instinct.

Everyone, from their first heartbeat, has a spirit that develops for better or worse over time. Jesus always drew his audience, so habitually focused on the externals, back to this spiritual fact of life. He said, "Yet a time is coming and has now come when the true worshipers must worship in the Spirit and in truth, for they are the kind of worshipers the Father seeks. God is spirit, and his worshipers must worship in the Spirit and in truth" (John 4:23-24).

In Jewish and Christian tradition, the terms *spirit, heart,* and *soul* are used to describe this unseen life with God. You might need to reclaim the meanings of these terms because they have been diluted and distorted over time. True meanings matter, however, because philosophies, parenting styles, and daily choices grow out of them.

In *Renovation of the Heart*, respected Christian author and philosophy professor Dallas Willard makes helpful distinctions:

Will is the *power* given by God to decide, act, and create.

Heart is the will's *location* as core to a person's being.

Spirit is the will's *essence* as nonphysical, unseen.

The will interplays with and is affected by all the other aspects of a human being—the *mind* (thoughts and feelings), *body*, and *social ties*—which collectively compose our entire being, the soul.[5] The beliefs and decisions of the will direct a person's life. It's what makes you *you*. But it is not the strongest component of your being, yet. You only begin to realize its potential and power when God is one with you there. And that requires your permission.

Christians of all backgrounds—Catholic, Orthodox, and Protestant—hold that the first step of faith is when a person decides to believe in God. "If you confess with your mouth that Jesus is Lord and believe in your heart that God raised him from the dead, you will be saved. For with the heart one believes and is justified, and with the mouth one confesses and is saved" (Romans 10:9-10, ESV). Through baptism, a person publicly dies to the old self and rises with the new self through the body of Christ. This is how one is born of water and the Spirit. It signifies a rebirth of promise now dedicated to a forgiven life that grows more like him.

The heart then becomes a home for the Holy Spirit, the Helper, who inspires the believer to declare, "not my will but yours, Lord" (Luke 22:42, John 14:15-23). This life with God can start in the very earliest years, as infants and toddlers grow up in an atmosphere of faith among their families, experiencing contentment as physical needs are met, developing a bond of trust with parents, and receiving acceptance from their loving eyes and words. Far from being a component to break, a child's will is the power God gave to become the unique individual he planned long ago, with God at the guiding center of it.

People who choose to exclude God from their hearts will plan and make decisions based on external circumstances, and so their hearts will be at the mercy of them. Their contentment then hinges on externals—earning a promotion at work, getting their body into shape, or going on exciting vacations. Then, they think, they will feel good about themselves and offer a happy life for their children.

But reliance on external factors can only take a soul so far. Promotions sometimes don't happen. Our bodies are never exactly what we want them to be. Vacations disappoint. The heated passions of romance fade under the day in, day out realities of life inside a marriage. The chores of being a new parent become physically and emotionally overwhelming. The underlying problems always surface. Tension builds as husband and wife negotiate for their share of time and money to meet their own needs. They can evolve into adversaries.

Most couples will unwittingly find themselves at this very place more than once. We all get distracted and challenged in life—materially, physically, and spiritually. Our reflex is to react with actions and words aimed at self-preservation. Priorities get out of whack.

Only belief in God and dwelling with him at our core, as originally intended, returns our being to its beneficially functioning order from the inside, out. When a will is one with God in the heart, all other aspects of a life—mind, body, and social interactions—transform over time, as the whole soul becomes more like him. Relationships transform, too.

The lifeblood of this God-centered, unseen life is not belief, however. It is love.

"If I have the gift of prophecy and can fathom all mysteries and all knowledge, and if I have a faith that can move mountains, but do not have love, I am nothing" (1 Corinthians 13:2). No amount of spiritual depth or breadth can overcome a lack of love.

It was in the midst of a harassed and helpless generation, completely at the mercy of external circumstances, that Jesus showed the way of selfless love, or *agape*, commanded by God (Matthew 9:35-36). For more than twenty centuries his worldwide revolution, this "Christ in me," has moved hearts to aspire and persevere to fulfill it. Is it any wonder we symbolize love with a heart?

As children dwell in families that understand their true human anatomy and their design for Jesus at the core, they stand a better chance of assimilating feelings of self-worth and love. They will still experience difficulties and detours in matters of love. But they will have a steady source—Christ's seal of love over their hearts, and the hearts of their mothers and fathers. In time, you become the most intimate and reliable of neighbors, right in your very own home.

Build & Grow

Learn

- Look up Mark 12:28-31 and write out the passage. Underline each separate command about love. Reflect on each command. Why do you think God has chosen these specific areas for us as "the most important?"

Absorb

- Reflect on your story about inviting Jesus into your heart. Are there any external matters that have less influence on you now?

Praise

- Identify a recent occasion when your spouse was loving in one of the ways commanded in Mark 12:28-31. Share with your spouse what you recall and give God your appreciation for the faithfulness.

Connect

- 1 Corinthians 13:4-8 gives us love's impressive resume. Commit with your spouse to memorizing these verses. Make it easier and more fun by quizzing one another, writing them on note cards, using a Bible memorization app, or just adding a couple of lines a week. Hiding these truths in your hearts as a couple is sure to enrich your marriage.

2. Set your heart on devotion

As the Father has loved me, so have I loved you. Now remain in my love. If you keep my commands, you will remain in my love, just as I have kept my Father's commands and remain in his love. I have told you this so that my joy may be in you and that your joy may be complete. My command is this: Love each other as I have loved you.

— JOHN 15:9-12

> Love for God and family starts with willful commitment, and it grows through good times and bad under God's loving care.

The pattern of the world is to find someone attractive to you, fall in love, have a passionate romance, host a wonderful wedding, and then enjoy those first few days because after that the honeymoon is over. Couples who have been married for a while likely will agree that the first year can be one of the hardest.

Part of the challenge for newly married couples today is the lack of preparation for such a major life change. We are largely left to our own devices in finding a spouse and deciding on marriage. We use visible and visceral cues, like a dating service profile, a friend's advice, or physical chemistry, in deciding whether to pursue commitment.

When the spark is there, we conclude it must be love.

"Today, people living in the Western world are supposed to marry for love. Considerable emphasis is placed on romance and human emotion," writes Hebrew and Bible expert Marvin R. Wilson. "The challenge each new couple always faces is how to mold this premarital feeling of romance into mature love."

For men and women of Bible times, Wilson continues, "Love was more a commitment than a feeling. It was seen foremost as a pledge rather than an emotional high. It was a person's good word to stick with someone, to make the relationship work," and then love deepened over time in marriage, with the backing and support of an extended family and the entire community.[6]

The pledge to stick with it, absent the emotional or physical high, was possible because marriages were pre-arranged and reinforced by the community. That's not something we want to go back to today. But within that structure, the expectation was that love would grow over the course of a life experienced together. The fabric of ancient Jewish society depended on it. Couples who feared and loved God made it so, as Marvin notes, following the example of Isaac and Rebekah (Genesis 24:67).[7]

The relationship with God takes a similar path of commitment first. A new believer commits to submitting to God's will and to following God's commandments. Such a commitment is not usually accompanied by an emotional high, but a sober recognition of our sinful, helpless state, and the promise from God that he will transform us as we walk with him. Then, with thousands of tiny steps in time and experiences with God, our love for him grows. It's our expectation. Our intimacy with God depends on it.

We can expect love to grow because creation is set up this way by God. Humans are dynamic spiritual beings who hunger for growth or they sink into complacency, despondency, or depression. That's why some born again Christians who had an emotionally charged conversion end up like the seed in shallow soil described by Jesus (Mark 4). They experienced the initial joy, but didn't understand the importance of devotion and growth in their relationship with God, and didn't cultivate the deeper roots that would help them endure hardship. The same is true in marriage and family.

We also can expect love to grow when we realize the meager share of it that we offer to begin with. Not because we are misers but because we haven't lived through enough yet. Far from chipping away at love's strength in a new marriage, difficulties in the first years are opportunities to exercise and expand love. We can expect love in marriages and families to grow because God, the source of love, has an unlimited amount to give to us if we will just receive it.

You witness the consequences when husband and wife are not devoted to one another in good times and bad, in sickness and health. To them, marriage was love's climax, not its starting point. They didn't foster roots. Each spouse must be able to endure challenging seasons in a marriage and devote time for the love of a family to grow. How sad to see that potential wither, go to waste, and then to see the impact of that failure multiplied in children's lives and subsequent generations.

Growing love is never an accident (Ephesians 4:16). It is the result of a heart's bent, and a willful decision to choose love and oneness over hate and division. If people "fall out of love" it is because they choose to out of pride, selfishness, or indifference. It can be a painfully easy choice or drift. The enemy, Satan and his legions, will give plenty of support for that bent.

On the other hand, if you devote yourself to choosing love and fostering its growth, then God and all the forces of Heaven are aligned to help you. Miraculously, simply praying for your love to grow, opens up the potential to make it so (Philippians 1:9, 1 Thessalonians 3:12).

But even the most loving marriages and parent-child relationships can experience rough times that the greatest devotion cannot fix. Don't go through such times alone. God designed humans to be interdependent. He equips Christian counselors who can help you recognize unhealthy issues or unloving patterns to which you might be totally blind. The process will cost time and emotion, but the healing God gives will change the direction of your life. After all, if God can love someone like us, so unmindful of him and undeserving, then truly anything is possible.

In the 1800s, Scottish reverend John Watson observed:

Love is the first and the last and the strongest bond in experience. It conquers distance, outlives all changes, bears the strain of the most diverse opinions. What a proof of Jesus' divine insight that he did not make his Church a school—whether the Temple or the porch—but a family; did not demand in his farewell that his disciples should think alike but that they should feel alike.[8]

A parent's heart filled with God's love will muster its power in the most difficult times, and a child will notice. All the while, God will grow the family's love, devotion, and gratitude for him, too.

Build & Grow

Learn

- Review Romans 12:9-12, choose one verse and describe how you can practically apply this to benefit your marriage and family.

Absorb

- If you remain devoted to your spouse and child, the passing years allow time for deep roots to develop. Describe another area of your life where you invested significant time or energy and experienced a tangible result.

Praise

- Reflect on a recent situation in your marriage when God blessed you with hope, patience, or an answered prayer. Write out a note of gratitude to God. Keeping an ongoing journal of prayers and praises to God is a valuable tool for drawing closer to him, developing your prayer life, and growing your faith.

Connect

- Don't leave your vows behind at the altar. Write them out together as a couple and display them in your home. They can serve as a daily reminder as you strive to fill your marriage and home with love. As your children grow, they will see you live out your vows and someday choose them as their own.

3. Know love's greatest strength

Greater love has no one than this:
to lay down one's life for one's friends.
—JOHN 15:13

When you devote yourself to loving God, he uses your acts of service and sacrifice to unlock your self-absorption and transform you. Service and sacrifice are profoundly spiritual acts using emotional and physical energy to magnify love and bond us in marriage and family.

When we were single and childless, we were constantly told by friends who had kids: "You have no idea how much everything changes!" Although we got tired of hearing that, and sometimes resented it, the truth was we really had no idea. And we couldn't have.

Getting married and having children is like stepping across two major thresholds that expose you to a whole new spiritual landscape of unimaginable depths and contours. You love more deeply and feel joy more deeply than you ever had before. You also hurt more deeply. For the first time in a long time, you realize how helpless you really are. You learn the limits of your control.

You also realize the tight hold that your own desires have on you, and that maybe, as C.S. Lewis suggested, our biggest struggle isn't to love God, but to love others as well as we love ourselves.[9] Do we extend the forgiveness and mercy and grace to others that we desire for ourselves? God offers a way for us.

Just as his physical laws manage outcomes in the physical world, so it is with life in the spiritual world. A profoundly mysterious truth of God's order is that service and sacrifice not only magnify love, but they also multiply it. People love the things they pour their emotional and physical energy into—whether a plant, a pet, a house, or a job. That's why even a person far from God can love others well. Service and sacrifice for another's good, such as the comfort of a child, reward one and all. This law is at work even while doing the lowliest tasks for others, such as changing a diaper, cooking a meal, or washing someone's tired feet. Jesus said we are blessed when we follow his example (John 13:1-17).

Serving others is very often rejuvenating. Hearts naturally swell. Ask men and women who serve and sacrifice in the military what motivates them, and they will often say "love of country." The longer they serve their country, the more they usually love it and their hard fought freedom. Few things are more poignant than seeing an aged veteran weep at a memorial.

In a speech at West Point in 1962, General Douglas MacArthur observed:

> The soldier, above all other men, is required to practice the greatest act of religious training—sacrifice. In battle and in the face of danger and death, he discloses those divine attributes, which his Maker gave when he created man in his own image. No physical courage and no brute instinct can take the place of the Divine help which alone can sustain him.[10]

The same is true with fathers and mothers. God uses service and sacrifice in the pathways of marriage and parenthood to unlock our prison of self-absorption. Such daily acts can be as small as putting down what we're doing and giving our child or spouse our full attention. And they can be as large as keeping hopeful vigil by a sickbed. Such acts of steady devotion serve God's plan of transformation in you. The result is a growing oneness with God and family members, just as Jesus prayed: "that all of them may be one, Father, just as you are in me and I am in you. May they also be in us" (John 17:20-21).

This unity of God is in fact the communion of Love.

In the Parable of the Good Samaritan (Luke 10:25-37), Jesus is answering the question, "Who is my neighbor?" But as always, his luminous story hits a multitude of cylinders with an unexpected twist. We are all thinking the neighbor is the man in the ditch, and we are there to help him. But rather than answering who a neighbor is, Jesus describes what a neighbor does. He asks, "Which of these three do you think was a neighbor to the man who fell into the hands of robbers?"

Ultimately the neighbor, the Samaritan, is Jesus. We know the lengths to which his love will go. We also see a basic spiritual truth at work that the personal cost of service and sacrifice is a supreme form of love, the best possible neighbor. And God himself demonstrates it for us in the highest. This is how, in a marriage and family, you can love more deeply and feel joy more deeply than you ever have before: You have plenty of immediate opportunities for service and sacrifice.

"You could never have felt the joy, nor had the faintest idea of what your love was, if that sacrifice had been denied you," Fulton J. Sheen writes. "But if your love were absent, then the sacrifice would have been a pain, vexation, and annoyance.

> The truth gradually emerges that our highest happiness consists in the feeling that another's good is purchased by our sacrifice; that the reason why pain is bitter is because we have no one to love and for whom we might suffer. Love is the only force in the world which can make pain bearable, and it makes it more than bearable by transforming it into the joy of sacrifice.[11]

When you devote yourself to loving God, your faithful friends service and sacrifice will do their work in your soul and your family. You can experience in marriage and parenting a love like God's that never fails.

Build & Grow

Learn

- Jesus said to his disciples, "Whoever wants to be my disciple must deny themselves and take up their cross and follow me. For whoever wants to save their life will lose it, but whoever loses their life for me will find it" (Matthew 16:24-25). Where do you see the message of sacrifice and service within this Scripture?

Absorb

- During the first years of marriage and building a new family, your spiritual life can take a hit before you realize it. Service and sacrifice can be a strain, so you must continually be refreshed. Just as you care for your body, establish a healthy spiritual diet to nourish your inner life. Your plan could include early morning walks alone, reading inspirational books, or listening to beautiful music.

  Your plan might also call for avoiding specific activities that cloud your soul, like certain kinds of entertainment, reading material, or topics of conversation. With thoughtful care for your family's spiritual nourishment looking ahead, you will notice a difference in your overall wellbeing and relationships.

Praise

- In what ways, big and small, do you see your spouse lovingly sacrifice for and serve you? Write it out and then share with your spouse how these acts make your feel about him or her.

Connect

- Having or adopting a child will consume a new mom and dad. It is during this time that you give others a great opportunity to show their love and serve you. Don't feel guilty! Gladly accept their help. Your stores of gratitude will fuel your service for future new parents when you are in a calmer season.

Plan Ahead

List three meaningful points from LOVE:

1.

2.

3.

Write a LOVE gift for your child:

Write a letter to your child, expressing your hopes about the kind of parent you will be. Make a commitment to nourish your child with unconditional love, and ask for forgiveness for mistakes you will make along the way. Going back and reading it at various stages in your child's life will remind you about your hopes and keep you on course. When the time is right, you can pass on this family heirloom to your child.

LOVE early childhood board book connections:
Jesus Shows Me and *Your Core*

Remember

This new phase in your life, as future-oriented as it tends to be, must be truthfully informed by the past and healthfully rooted in it. Time—history— is a friend to faith. In fact, having a child-like faith, which pleases Jesus, requires continually remembering how God has revealed himself in human history and in our lives personally.

Newborn Fact of Life

Your child has great capacity for faith.
Your family life will shape it.

Compelling research today gives us a bigger appreciation for how the miraculous brain works in the first months of life, already weaving impressions and memories. We know that the amount and variety of words spoken to an infant, and the richness of loving, familial experiences have a cascading positive influence on cognitive and emotional development.[1]

At your newborn's first check-up, the doctor will likely instruct you to start reading to your child right away, as recommended by the American Academy of Pediatrics.[2] Others in the political, educational, and industrial sectors have carved out niches to take advantage of this important developmental window. Why do companies target early childhood for marketing their products? Your child's mindshare is of great interest to other grownups.

But the first days and years of life involve more than the gray matter. As Christians, we know these little think tanks have spirits, too, because they are made in God's image. All children, no matter what their condition, have a spiritual life. A child has the capacity to develop faith from the beginning in the setting of family life and community. Impressions are made, and we know from our own experiences that they last a lifetime.

Thomas F. Torrance, a 20th century Protestant theologian well regarded for his works on science, writes:

> A child by the age of five has learned, we are told, an astonishing amount about the physical world to which he or she has become spontaneously and intuitively adapted—far more than the child could ever understand if he or she turned out to be the most brilliant of physicists. Likewise, I believe, we learn far more about God as Father, Son, and Holy Spirit, into whose Name we have been baptized, within the family and fellowship and living tradition of the Church than we can ever say: It becomes built into the structure of our souls and minds, and we know much more than we can ever tell.[3]

All people throughout their lives continually accept ideas as reliable truths without being able to explain them—or even see them. Just think about gravity. A. W. Tozer observed, "Every man lives by faith, the nonbeliever as well as the saint; the one by faith in natural laws and the other by faith in God."[4]

How much faith can a child have? Plenty. God has made the most important facts about him the easiest to apprehend. And to further help us along, he made the New Covenant through Jesus and the gift of the Holy Spirit, so that we may know him personally:

> I will put my law in their minds and write it on their hearts. I will be their God, and they will be my people. No longer will a man teach his neighbor, or a man his brother, saying, 'Know the Lord.' Because they will all know me, from the least of them to the greatest, declares the Lord (Jeremiah 31:33-34).

We can share with children sweeping thoughts about God such as spirit, power, sacrifice, Heaven, and eternity because their hearts are intuitively set to receive them. Enriching your child now prepares him for receiving deeper spiritual truths as he grows.[5]

Conventional wisdom holds that young children cannot absorb meanings about things they cannot see. But the real challenge is an adult's ability to communicate under the scrutiny of a child's exacting nature for detail. Children are literalists.

One pastor related his confusion as a child with the hymn "I'll be a Sunbeam." He wondered why Jesus wanted him to be a sunbeam. A child came to her mother concerned because she thought "I shall not want" in the KJV of Psalm 23:1 meant that it was a sin for her to want anything. The mealtime prayer actually does sound like, "lettuce thank him for our food." Have some fun and laugh together about things like that. Children are capable, at their humble age, of accepting God's truth as a reality that makes sense. Jesus said we must all approach faith this way (Matthew 18:3).

> "It becomes built into the structure of our souls and minds, and we know much more than we can ever tell."
>
> —Thomas F. Torrance

The sheep of Jesus know his voice (John 10). As babies' ears are new to this world and their hearts like soft wax, let your desire be to share Jesus' words because his children will recognize him. The power of the Word is unexplainable in human terms, but there it is. God's words will not fail in his purpose for them, a promise fulfilled throughout Scripture and time.

What Remembering Can Do in Marriage & Family

Praise the LORD, O my soul;
* all my inmost being, praise his holy name.*
Praise the LORD O my soul,
* and forget not his benefits—*
who forgives all your sins
* and heals all your diseases,*
who redeems your life from the pit
* and crowns you with love and compassion,*
who satisfies your desires with good things
* so your youth is renewed like the eagle's.*

—PSALM 103:1-5

One of the first impacts of becoming a parent is memory loss. It's true! Fluctuating hormones, sleep deprivation, and caring for a newborn are mentally and physically consuming. Your mind scatters. Just chalk it up to mommy and daddy brain. Everyone who has ever been there will understand, if they can remember it.

With that, however, it's all the more important to exercise in advance of parenthood (or as soon as your capacity returns) your ability *to remember.* A whole new chapter in life with fresh pages awaits you, and this promising future finds its greatest wisdom and strength in the past—God's and yours.

This new phase in your life, as future-oriented as it tends to be, must be truthfully informed by the past and healthfully rooted in it. Time—history—is a friend to faith. Immersion in God's past, and remembering how he has revealed himself in actual events of human history, enables you to witness his plan unfold for all time. It gives perspective and meaning to your own past, as you reflect on God's active role in it.

You might be exploring faith after many years of drifting from God, and now on the parenting threshold, you are thinking seriously about him for the first time in a long time. Maybe you never fully knew him. Or, your soul, long connected with Christ, is now stirred by other unnamed yearnings for your future child.

When planning for a family, a common desire is to make a better life for our children than we had, not to repeat the harm or mistakes of our parents, and to carry forward treasured experiences from our childhood and make them even better, if possible.

God himself inspires such desire in those who put their faith in him. He is a God of transformation. "I will give them an undivided heart and put a new spirit in them; I will remove from them their heart of stone and give them a heart of flesh" (Ezekiel 11:19). God's gifts of marriage and parenting are refineries for living hearts. Remembering is the tool God gave you for that process.

Remembering sifts and distills. It assimilates beneficial changes. It spurs growth. Because God is unseen, remembering is your means for dwelling in his presence and gaining understanding about him. It is an ability God actually shares with us. As we are called to remember him, he pledges to remember us. Remembering, then, is the active vehicle for a deeply intimate life with God.

From Genesis to Revelation more than 300 promises, requests, and commandments in the Bible emphasize the importance of *remember-*

ing and *not forgetting*. Over and over we encounter passages such as, "Only be careful, and watch yourselves closely so that you do not forget the things your eyes have seen or let them fade from your heart as long as you live" (Deuteronomy 4:9).

Perhaps for every time God enjoins us to remember him, the heart of humankind cries back to be remembered. Far from being a passive act, remembering for God and people holds specific meaning that calls for action. By pledging to remember his covenants, God vows to act on them, and we know from experience that he has. God didn't need Moses to remind him of his covenant. In faith, Moses asked God to act on it, and God faithfully responded:

> *Moses said to the Lord, "You have been telling me, 'Lead these people,' but you have not let me know whom you will send with me. You have said, 'I know you by name and you have found favor with me.' If you are pleased with me, teach me your ways so I may know you and continue to find favor with you. Remember that this nation is your people." The Lord replied, "My Presence will go with you, and I will give you rest"* (Exodus 33:12-14).

When Jesus entered this world as the Son of Man, he came as an infant, who would grow along with his own memories. Jesus used his faculty of remembering as a lifeline to his Father, one that helped him resist any temptation and sustained his steady path to the Cross (Matthew 4, John 19). We have the same lifeline. Remembering God—his divine attributes, his providence, his reliability, and his commands—can be the difference between our utter failure and divine deliverance. Remembering God is also one of the greatest forms of demonstrating love for him. Likewise, God demonstrates great love for you by *remembering*.

The last recorded words spoken to Jesus on the Cross were a plea by the criminal next to him: "Jesus, remember me when you come into your Kingdom." Jesus replied, "Today, you will be with me in paradise" (Luke 23:39-43).

A sharper awareness of your past and God's presence in it will give you an honest perspective on your life, setting up a truly strong, sure-footed beginning for your family. Here are just three ways that remembering can impact the new chapter that awaits you:

Remembering strengthens faith. The cost of forgetting or even passively drifting away in your faith through neglect is high, and far too easy to do when the immediate demands of physical life take precedence. The task of remembering is especially important to the faith in new marriages and families encountering so many "firsts" in one season.

Within mere decades of Jesus' presence on earth, the author of the book of Hebrews sounded strong warnings to early Christians about the effects of their forgetting: spiritual drift, hardness of heart, dullness, and worst of all apostasy or unbelief. The author's inspired remedy was a passionate enjoiner for believers to remember who they are in Christ, to remember God's acts in Israel's history, and to remember the heroes of the faith who came before them so they, too, can persevere and not lose heart. The entire New Testament reverberates the same theme and urgency.

Jesus said, "Therefore, remember what you have received and heard; hold fast, and repent" (Revelation 3:3). Don't forget where you came from and the treasure you hold. Don't be sidetracked by the many distractions in this life. In all seasons, remembering will reinforce your faith.

Remembering strengthens renewal. While you mature and grow as a disciple of Jesus, your awareness of God's work in your past will continue to come into focus. Looking back with a spirit-guided lens, you can notice and learn from your past, especially the bad times and mistakes.

We all fall short. And though we are forgiven through Christ, we live with consequences of our own sin or someone else's (Romans 3:23-24). In a process over time, God will peel back layers and connect truths from your past that are important to your spiritual health and maturity going forward. "He heals the brokenhearted and binds up their wounds" (Psalm 147:3).

God's power to help you overcome terrible or unfortunate past events is infinite. He will even use them for your good (Romans 8:28). How can you access this promise? You spend time with him reflecting. You also reach out to a person you trust for support. God's gentle mercies in healing you will humble you and melt your heart of stone:

> *When my heart was grieved*
> *and my spirit embittered,*
> *I was senseless and ignorant;*
> *I was a brute beast before you.*
> *Yet I am always with you;*
> *You hold me by my right hand.*
> *You guide me with your counsel,*
> *And afterward you will take me into glory.*
> —PSALM 73:21-24

Remembering strengthens identity. You begin your new phase of Christian life with a spiritual heritage based on knowledge passed down through thousands of years by faithful generations. Your family's spiritual identity and experiences then become part of your child's inheritance, and that of generations to follow. Spiritual life has always worked this way. To appreciate these ripple effects of faith since the beginning of humankind, read the grand display in Hebrews 11.

The bedrock of Christian spiritual parenting is helping your child to remember God's activity in the past, which gives context for his activity in the present and builds trust in his promised activity in the future (Deuteronomy 6). You establish a child's spiritual identity and the expectation of a personal calling in God's design (Ephesians 2). Remembering God forms the basis of an active, hands-on life with him at any age. It frames and reinforces our self-image and our long-planned role in his design.

"This concept of history brings ultimate meaning and purpose to both personal and global events," Bible scholar Marvin R. Wilson writes. "We are not alone. The future is secure. God is alive, at work, and in control."[6]

Applying It in Marriage and Family Life

Isn't it just like God to inspire your brand new life with the full force of the past? He knows what you need. In the following sections, you will:

- **Re-parent your soul.** Carry the child you once were into your new journey and find a measure of love and grace not yet known to you.

- **Survey your spiritual roots.** Get a full picture of your roots in faith and your position in the family of Jesus.

- **Remember not to forget.** Determine to use remembering as a guiding force for ever-growing ties with your loving Creator.

In the Christian walk, our past does not bog us down nor defeat us. It becomes an instrument in our evolving Christ-likeness amid an ever-renewing present. "Because of the Lord's great love we are not consumed, for his compassions never fail. They are new every morning; great is your faithfulness" (Lamentations 3:22-23). Each new dawn delivers God's promise for your newborn spirit.

1. Re-parent your soul

When [Jesus] saw the crowds, he had compassion on them, because they were harassed and helpless, like sheep without a shepherd.

—MATTHEW 9:36

> Whatever the scope of your memories, remembering helps you identify and name previous facts and feelings, put them in their proper place, and decide how they will inform your life today and tomorrow.

Perhaps no life change triggers more memories than becoming a parent. Parenthood starts a revolution in the soul, where childhood memories barrel from the past, adding to the haze of mommy and daddy brain. This benevolent crisis, the collision of past and present, is a gift from God. It can benefit you, your marriage, and your child in many ways if you allow it to do so.

Upon becoming a first-time mother, one friend was physically sickened when she thought about drinking wine in front of her baby. It brought to mind her own mother's alcoholism, which was aided by her silent, accommodating family. Our friend sought support for the first time ever to resolve her unexamined, crippling memories.

Whatever the scope of your memories, remembering helps you to identify and name previous facts and feelings, put them in their proper place, and decide how they will inform your life today and tomorrow.

Your first two decades of life were largely determined by other people who decided where you would live and go to school, what family life would be like, and how you would spend your time. Many people can attest to having wonderful parents or guardians in those years, but none can claim to have had perfect ones. It's just not humanly possible.

If you married in a church, you might have already taken pre-marital classes or counseling that explored your families of origin. Getting family history out on the table can be a huge step in identifying unresolved issues that might impact a marriage. Sorting through a few of the tangles now will also clear the path for the parent that you will become, that your child needs you to be.

Here at the threshold of parenting, soul searching is a practical application of remembering. With a broad sweep, reflect over the years of your life, with its periods of happiness, sadness, tragedy, and joy. Certain people, events, achievements, and regrets are bound to stand out.

Your experience is the human experience. The Bible charts such highs and lows with oftentimes painful clarity through hundreds of actual names and events. But for all the wickedness and vile behavior examined there, God's inspired Word holds out an extraordinary alternative for another way: "Behold, I am doing a new thing; now it springs forth, do you not perceive it? I will make a way in the wilderness and rivers in the desert" (Isaiah 43:19).

> "Forgiving does not erase the bitter past. A healed memory is not a deleted memory. Instead, forgiving what we cannot forget creates a new way to remember."
> —Lewis B. Smedes

As an adult you are now responsible for the child you once were. Becoming a parent gives you a new perspective on the patterns that have taken shape throughout your life and the opportunity to alter

Examining family history can be very painful and unearth memories or feelings that need to be processed with a professional counselor. Contact your church or family doctor for referrals, and know that any steps you take toward healing will benefit all of your significant relationships.

your course. Everything you learn about parenting also can be applied to the child you once were. Did you have an aloof parent? Well, here you are now holding your child and deciding, "that won't happen here anymore."

God can build upon your positive memories and transform the hard and ugly ones into something beautiful for your family. Thousands of years of human experience with a very personal God testify to it. Remember: He "heals the brokenhearted and binds up their wounds" (Psalm 147:30). With God's help, you can re-parent your soul.

Extend the love and compassion you have for your new child to the child you once were, and who is still very much a part of you. It will be a healing balm for past wounds. It will kindle your forgiveness, and so prevent you from passing on bitter roots to your children, instead stopping such generational strongholds.

Ours is the God of healing, and this God gives you as a parent a new start, right along with your child. Pray over the feelings that come up and ask for help identifying where forgiveness is needed. In time, you will be amazed as God peels away the years and lightens an unnameable load (Psalm 103:5). You will find a measure of love and grace not yet known to you. You will freely pass it on.

Build & Grow

Learn

- Write out Psalm 147:3 and Ezekiel 11:19. In your own words, what does God offer to his people? Which verse do you identify with the most and why?

Absorb

- Here at the threshold of parenting, soul searching is a practical application of remembering. With a broad sweep, reflect over the years of your life, with its periods of happiness, sadness, tragedy, and joy. Certain events, achievements, regrets, and high points are bound to stand out. Reflect over your life in 5 years increments: age 0-5, age 6-10, age 11-15, and age 16-20. Give yourself ample time and write out short phrases that capture key memories.

Praise

- It's all too easy to focus on the negative aspects of our past and present. Sometimes stepping back and getting perspective on the tender mercies and kindnesses along the way can strengthen renewal and restore hope.

You can reinforce your positive memories by sharing them with others. Circle specific things from your Absorb list above that you appreciated about your childhood. Notice which ones you can carry forward with your own child.

Some families remember God's goodness by sharing spiritually meaningful moments on Christmas ornaments, placing them in a jar annually, and writing them on garden stones. Do what works best for your family and that which ultimately sparks rich conversation with your child and future generations.

Connect

- Exchange with your spouse the top one or two aspects of your pasts in need of healing. For example, would you like to be healed from too much criticism in your past? Was love in your childhood based on performance? Review your circumstances through a new God-filtered perspective and his desires for you.

Identify a few areas where re-parenting your soul could be helpful, such as by showing love, using discipline, being truthful, establishing healthy routines, giving affirmation, or creating a home of trust, unity, loyalty, and respect.

Together, pray for one another about any areas uncovered in the questions above. Consider whether any other steps would be helpful for healing, such as Christian counseling, and discuss how you can support one another in this growth.

2. Survey your spiritual roots

And I pray that you, being rooted and established in love, may have the power, together with all the Lord's holy people, to grasp how wide and long and high and deep is the love of Christ, and to know this love, which surpasses knowledge—that you may be filled to the measure of all the fullness of God.

—EPHESIANS 3:17-19

> Our first impressions of God come from our family of origin. But we have deep spiritual roots that go back thousands of years—all Christians do. We benefit when we remember them.

When Christians tell their personal story of faith, they usually begin with their family of origin. The first years in life establish our first impressions of God and set the course for our experience with him.

Did your family attend church and profess belief, but lived another way during the week? Were religious heritage and tradition more important than an actual relationship with the Lord? Did you grow up in a home of passive faith that was expected to transfer to you through osmosis? Or maybe your home was unbelieving, openly indifferent or hostile to God.

Before you were married, you very likely discussed your spiritual background with your future spouse. However, as you prepare for your new parenting roles, it is a good time for you both to remember together the specific family experiences that exposed you to faith. Each of you will need to assess any bias, assumptions, or lack of information you have about how spiritual life is shared, experienced, and taught. Because let's face it: we all have some spiritual baggage that can impact our view of God and the view that we naturally pass on to our children.

Seemingly benign past experiences infiltrate our current mindset. Maybe your aunt with bad breath and unstylish clothes was a Bible thumper and bugged you about attending church every time you saw her. Would it color your interest in that faith? And usually our earthly father, for better or worse, is who we think of when we hear the words "Our Father." For a husband, "Father God," might naturally remind him of a generous and kind-hearted family man. But for a wife, "Father God," might bring up an image of a strict disciplinarian whose love is earned only through achievement and success.

Childhood memories imprint our souls and shape all aspects of the people we become over the course of our lives. An honest look at your own spiritual history will help you as a parent and spouse. A new husband and wife who acknowledge to one another their disappointments, confusion, and fond memories, will stand a better chance of setting a thoughtful course for their own family's faith. It is a watershed season of life for husband, wife, and new child—and an opportunity exquisitely primed by God.

We know that love is vital to our well being from birth. We know that children are born to believe and are innately attuned to loving God, who sets their hearts on eternity (Ecclesiastes 3:11). We know their faith has a purpose: "Through the praise of children and infants you have established a stronghold against your enemies, to silence the foe and the avenger" (Psalm 8:2). And we know that children who believe in God in childhood and commit their lives to Jesus make up a large majority of adult believers today.[7]

It appears that, other than our parents, no relationship is shaped more by early childhood than our relationship with God. It is only with him in view that we can overcome the shortcomings of earthly parents. It's understandable, then, that the Bible from start to finish hammers on remembering him. Jewish scholar Yosef Hayim Yerushalmi observes:

> When God introduces himself directly to the entire people at Sinai, nothing is heard of his essence or attributes, but only: "I the Lord am your God who brought you out of the land of Egypt, the house of bondage" (Exodus 20:2). That is sufficient. For here as elsewhere, ancient Israel knows what God is from what he has done in history. And if that is so, then memory has become crucial to its faith and, ultimately, to its very existence.[8]

"Therefore, as you received Christ Jesus the Lord, so walk in him, rooted and built up in him and established in the faith, just as you were taught, abounding in thanksgiving."

—Colossians 2:6-7

The same is true for you. Over and above your personal history with faith, you have deep spiritual roots that go back thousands of years—all Christians do. We have been grafted into the family of God through the work of Jesus (Ephesians 2:12-13). We forget the significance of this history at our peril.

In Romans 11, Paul explains how believing Gentiles, as "wild olive shoots," are brought near to the family of God by being "grafted in among the others and now share in the nourishing sap from the olive root" (verse 17). That's an amazing heritage we have gained!

Your past, present, and future—and your child's—are secure, because the life source of the root is God's unlimited love (Ephesians 3:16-19).

As you move through your days, take heed to this life-giving command from the Bible and *remember*. We are firmly rooted in the hope and love of God's chosen people, now as his chosen people, too. We do well to stay connected with that history, while examining our own past and remembering God's part in it all.

Build & Grow

Learn

- Some of us identify closely with our family of origin, while others have very few family ties. Regardless, the idea of "rootlessness" should be a foreign concept to a Christian, who has been grafted into the family of God through the work of Jesus. Read Ephesians 3:1-6. Since we are "rooted" in the family of God, the Bible can also be viewed as an account of our spiritual ancestors. Name a happening in the Bible that involves a person with whom you identify.

Absorb

- As Christians, we are firmly rooted in the ideas, teaching, traditions, hopes, and love of God's chosen people as his people now, too. Spiritually we are all adopted into the family of God. Read through Romans 8. Take some time to think about your spiritual roots—including how you met God, how his love changed you, how he's helped in you in hard times, ways he has guided you to find purpose, and miracles you've seen him perform along the way.

Praise

- Read the prayer in Ephesians 3:14-19 by the apostle Paul. Notice which family he refers to in verse 15. Pray this loving prayer as a blessing over your new family.

Connect

- How have Christian friends and your home church provided the benefits of family? Take some time to remember those who have had the most positive impact on you and how. Write a letter to give gratitude for what was done and the ways you benefited from acts or words they invested in you. Consider sending the letter. You might reconnect with someone dear to you.

3. Remember not to forget

The Spirit of the Lord is on me, because he has anointed me to proclaim good news to the poor. He has sent me to proclaim freedom for the prisoners and recovery of sight for the blind, to set the oppressed free, to proclaim the year of the Lord's favor.

—Luke 4:18-19

> We carry a habit of willful forgetting into adulthood because it often achieves our goal. Willful forgetting allows a person to slide by focusing on external or superficial matters, while neglecting the condition of the true inner self.

When you were growing up, did you ever forget to pick up your toys, brush your teeth, comb your hair, or say thank you?

You'll likely find out what it means to repeat something "until you are blue in the face," when you become a parent. Maybe your parents used that expression with you. Ours did! As kids, we usually had to be reminded—trained—to think about what we needed to do to take care of ourselves. Oftentimes we intentionally ignored a task because it interrupted play or something else we preferred instead.

We carry a habit of willful forgetting into adulthood because it often achieves our goal. Willful forgetting allows a person to slide by with self-centered or superficial matters, while ignoring the true inner condition and care for it. As an adult, it's easy to put on a good façade with a beautiful family, professional status, athletic ability, nice clothes, or charming personality. People like to be around other people with those qualities, so those qualities are socially rewarded.

But willful forgetting is also the easiest way for life to run off the rails. It is detrimental to the inner condition and permits wrongdoing, big and small, as people push thoughts of God out of their minds and ignore him. They wind up on a path to desolation, forgetting the wonders that God has done and continues to do all around. Herein lies their downfall. Especially for new parents who are still sorting out their married life and now have the demands of caring for an infant.

You could sum up the Bible and humankind's history with God by writing: They remembered; they forgot; they remembered; they forgot; they remembered; they forgot. You get the idea. When we read about the Israelite's self-inflicted wandering in the desert for 40 years, we should keep in mind that we are right there with them.

Works in progress that we are, we all have seasons of being stubborn and prideful in our dealings with God, forgetting to revere, obey, and love him. We mete out punishment to those around us or advance our own agenda by "forgetting" to do or say something that would benefit them.

Perhaps the most famous forgetter—and rememberer—in the Bible is the Prodigal Son, described in a parable by Jesus recorded in Luke 15. The son disrespected his father by demanding his inheritance and then left his home to squander it living "the good life." He willfully put behind the riches of his roots—his loving family ties, the plentiful provision of his father, and the cooperative community surrounding him. As a spectator, we can see where this is going. Reduced to hunger and the most menial, filthy work, the son was in the literal pit.

A turning point for him was the dawning of truth about his circumstances: he remembered the security of life at his father's house. This sent a shockwave through his soul—a benevolent crisis. Jesus tells us the son "came to himself" (verse 17). He remembered that even the servants in his father's house lived well.

At this point, the lost son determined he would go back to confess his unworthiness and offer himself as a servant. But as he approached, before he could even say a word, his father ran out to embrace him and welcome him home. The love of the father saved him. "Let's have a feast and celebrate," the father said, treating his returning son as an honored guest. "For this son of mine was dead and is alive again; he was lost and is found" (verses 23, 24). That's *our* Father.

We don't find out how the son fares throughout the rest of his earthly life. But those of us who are experiencing the journey of a saved soul can imagine that he still had ups and downs. His memory would serve him well, though, as would the humility and love he gained. He might have even made amends with his older brother, who refused to welcome him home. He, too, had willfully suppressed recalling the father's kind and extensive love.

At the beginning of his ministry, Jesus plainly announced his purpose in coming (Luke 4:18-19 noted above). Then, he succeeded in his mission to demolish the oppressive stranglehold of brokenness and sin in the lives of those who would believe in him. At his last meal, Jesus instructed his disciples to continually remember what he had done and was about to finish on the Cross. "And he took the bread, gave thanks and broke it, and gave it to them, saying, 'This is my body given for you; do this in remembrance of me'" (Luke 22:19).

The daily remembrance of God and what he has done in our lives impacts our whole being for all time. With each passing day our unique spiritual history accumulates, a history that grows lighter and lighter under the freedom Jesus secured for God's family. It will always be part of us, while becoming part of our children and their children. We must remember not to forget.

Build & Grow

Learn

- Willful forgetting is the easiest way for life to run off the rails. It is detrimental to the inner condition and permits wrongdoing—big and small—as people push thoughts of God out of their minds and ignore him. Review Jesus' parable of the Prodigal Son in Luke 15. Does this story fit more into your past or in your present? What part of the text do you identify with most?

Absorb

- The cost of forgetting or even passively drifting away in your faith through neglect is high, and far too easy to do with the many physical distractions in life. What spiritually healthy habits help you combat forgetting about God and nurture your faith?

Praise

- Acknowledge to God an area of your life today where you intentionally forget him. Ask him for forgiveness and for his help in changing course. Thank him for always remembering you.

Connect

- Decide now to build a spiritual heritage of remembering God in your family. Consider your strengths, spiritual gifts, and interests as a place to start. Some of your fondest memories could become praying at home together, or going out and serving those in need, or showing hospitality that builds your faith community. Your intentional choices for faith building can impact the family's spiritual life now and become your most influential legacy.

Plan Ahead

Choose points about REMEMBER to carry with you:

1.

2.

3.

Write a REMEMBER gift for your child:

Since your words as a parent have enormous power in shaping your child's spiritual heritage, write a blessing, poem, or song for your child and memorize it. Recite it to your child from the first day on—daily, weekly, or traditional times like birthdays. This will help everyone in the family remember the child's worth to you and Jesus. For inspiration read Numbers 6:24-26, the first priestly blessing recorded in Scripture.

REMEMBER early childhood board book connections:
All of Me That You Can't See and *To The Sea*

Seek

A soul must be sustained by its Source. Seeking is the steady exertion we make to affirm and grow our intimacy with God. We discover in the process that our spiritual thirst protects us from complacency, distraction, or unbelief, and develops a pattern our children will follow.

Newborn Fact of Life

> Your child has a one-of-a-kind path.
> You are a shepherd.

Young children have a way of confounding the experts. A mother and father struggling to get an infant to sleep might consult four or five different books with different methods—to no avail. Often a behavior will surface that doesn't quite fit any scenario in any survival guide. It's a *parenting* fact of life: Your child is a unique individual on a one-of-a-kind path. That must mean something to God.

"I am considering not how, but why, he makes each soul unique," C. S. Lewis writes. "If he had no use for all these differences, I do not see why he should have created more souls than one."[1]

Each soul—the collection of our thoughts, feelings, intuition, experiences, and memories—is endowed with a will. That decision-maker, the will, is in essence your child's spiritual being. It's how people create and move in the world with their gifts and talents, and it's our path to God, who has gone to great lengths to give humans a free will. So if we have free will with God, we have free will with our parents.

Skilled shepherds cannot force a lamb to live their preferred way.

A child cannot be forced to eat or sleep. Every parent experiences moments of complete exasperation in the face of a child's God-given will. God understands. A child cannot be forced to obey God either. Fortunately, God made it almost impossible for children not to love their parents. And, so, parents have great influence on those hearts of soft wax.

Christian parents are bound to encounter a child's free will when it comes to matters of faith. This is where we take on the mantle of the shepherd and begin helping children navigate the rewards and consequences of their choices.

The life of a shepherd is one constantly on alert looking out for the flock, aware and involved, but never intrusive or overbearing. He doesn't need to put his sheep on a leash. He knows sheep only follow a shepherd they trust, not one they fear. Sheep will even trust an appropriately bred and trained dog, but they will never trust a wolf.

The phrase "Your rod and your staff, they comfort me," in Psalm 23, reflects the peace of the shepherd's instruments of guidance, protection, and support. Jesus is the one Good Shepherd, a liberator of souls. Read his own words in John 10 to meditate on the depths of his love and the sacrificial acts involved in carrying that mantle.

> "He tends his flock like a shepherd: He gathers the lambs in his arms and carries them close to his heart; he gently leads those that have young."
> —Isaiah 40:11

The human limits of shepherding are laid bare for all to see, even the little lambs. The life of a shepherd is a humbling life. And your humble walk will be part of your witness to your child. During this time with you, as you seek and learn to walk with Jesus *your* Shepherd, your children join you, worshipping at church, praying and forgiving in every circumstance, reading the Bible, and learning to walk in his ways, too.

As you nurture and guide, you offer your child the safety to mark out a unique journey at your side. Your belief that God will do what he says he will do—and the hope for the eternity that goes with that—become vital, along with continual patience and prayer.

Holding your child out to God in prayer and gratitude is a powerful, meaningful way to love your child no matter where the journey leads or what the circumstances are. Sometime in your child's life you will be desperate to help him or her. Prayer will be your only hope. In prayer, you link with God in his great love and purpose for the child he made through you. A parent's prayers matter.

It's through prayer, in spirit, that the unique journey of your soul intertwines with the unique journey of your child's soul within the triune life of God. As Jesus prayed just before his crucifixion, "I have given them the glory that you gave me, that they may be one as we are one—I in them and you in me—so that they may be brought to complete unity" (John 17:22-23).

Our one-of-a-kind paths lead our souls to their place in eternity as God planned long ago (Psalm 139). One day we will dwell with God together in the fullness of our unique spirits for all eternity. There, you are promised a new name, which only you and God will know (Revelations 2:17). Meanwhile, we have Heaven on earth, God's Kingdom among us, to personally guide and keep us.

What Seeking Can Do in Marriage & Family

The Lord your God is in your midst,
a mighty one who will save;
he will rejoice over you with gladness;
he will quiet you by his love;
he will exult over you with loud singing.
—ZEPHANIAH 3:17, ESV

Education, innovation, prosperity—the story of progress in human history is the story of seeking. We seem to be wired to seek like we are wired to breathe. Is it possible that God withholds so much about himself so that we exercise our ability to seek *him*? That the yearning or need behind the seeking is the point? If we look at God's creation, the answer is *yes*.

A tree has a need for water, which spurs its roots to go deeper to find it. With a fully developed and thriving root system, a tree is strong and lives a long life. It withstands storms and revels in changing seasons. With a continual source to meet its thirst, the tree becomes what it was created to be.

When a buried seed splits, the sprout inside must push through the soil to seek sunlight for nourishment. If the sprout remained underground, it would not survive to become the beautiful plant that God designed.

The same is true of spiritual life, "for earth and heaven are twin parts of his works. And as the same law, so the same order prevails in them, and they form a grand unity in their relation to the living God who reigns."[2] As with the natural world, spiritual growth develops in subtle shapes and shades that are imperceptible to the human eye. Then one day, as if overnight, a huge transformation has arrived. A tree is in full flower. A baby is a child. A soul is at home with God.

Like a flower needing energy from the sun and nutrients from the rain, a spirit must be sustained by its Source. Such a spirit that seeks God truly finds him, and receives a reward so unearthly and affirming that it fuels more seeking of him. On and on the roots grow—*love* grows. You will sense God's delight over you, as beautifully stated in Zephaniah 3:17.

It's remarkable to see how quickly a strong, healthy life will die without the water it needs. An ignored thirst will kill a tree or sprout. Without the *need* to seek and the *will* to do it, a spiritual journey withers and dies, too. But here, the similarities with the rest of creation end. Unlike a tree, our spirits have potential to grow forever because they are eternal.

If change is an indication of physical life, then it must be especially so of spiritual life and the ties that bind God, our marriage, and our family. Relationships benefit when they evolve and grow.

While loving and remembering infuse the here and now, seeking stretches us toward the future and builds hope for it. Seeking is the steady exertion we make to affirm and grow our intimacy with God, gradually walking toward our future life, as we plant one foot here and now in his presence. We discover that in the process, our spiritual thirst protects us from complacency, distraction, or functional unbelief.

Meanwhile, you change more into God's likeness as you go. The immediate reward of finding God, your Promised Land, is enjoying intimacy with him today, and knowing more fully his great love, which is better than life (Psalm 63:3). The impact on you and your family cannot be described in human terms.

With spirits bent on seeking God, a mom and dad never run out of hope. New possibilities and spiritual discoveries are always around the corner. The unknowns of life transform into a confident Known, because we are continually in touch with our benevolent Teacher. Seeking brings surety, a faith that understands what cannot be seen. It grows our desire to know God more, deepening our roots in him. We withstand the storms and revel in the changing seasons. Here are just a few of the many fruits of seeking:

Seeking results in finding. Have you ever met anyone who earnestly sought God and didn't find him? Far from it: God himself draws us near to him, and so certainly we will find him. "All those the Father gives me will come to me," Jesus said, "and whoever comes to me I will never drive away" (John 6:37, see also verse 44), and "Come near to God and he will come near to you" (James 4:8).

What's more, God actively seeks us. "For the Son of Man came to seek and to save the lost" (Luke 19:10), and "I revealed myself to those who did not ask for me; I was found by those who did not seek me. To a nation that did not call on my name, I said, 'Here am I, here am I'" (Isaiah 65:1).

All Christians have a story about finding or being found by God. In Acts we meet an Ethiopian in this circumstance. He had been to Jerusalem to worship and had obtained a Greek copy of the book of Isaiah (seeking!). God faithfully had sown the first seed. Then, God arranged for him an encounter with the evangelist Philip. "Do

> "And their eyes were opened, and they recognized him. And he vanished from their sight. They said to each other, 'Did not our hearts burn within us while he talked to us on the road, while he opened to us the Scriptures?'"
> —Luke 24:31-32 (ESV)

you understand what you are reading?" Philip asked. "How can I," the Ethiopian said, "unless someone explains it to me?" The Ethiopian invited Philip in to teach him. He received God's Word, and then dedicated his life to Christ right then and there (Acts 8:26-39).

God stirred the Ethiopian's yearnings and met them. Human history teems with such testimonies of seeking and finding God, or being sought and found by him. Like the husband or wife of your dreams, when you find God, you know it. He meets you in unmistakably tailored ways.

Seeking results in wisdom. Just like your search for understanding marriage, pregnancy, and parenting, your search for understanding God gives you knowledge and wisdom for everyday life. God tells us that all we have to do is seek:

Yes, if you cry out for discernment, and lift up your voice for understanding, if you seek her as silver, and search for her as for hidden treasures; then you will understand the fear of the LORD, and find the knowledge of God (Proverbs 2:3-5, NKJV).

A good chunk of Proverbs emphatically elaborates on the necessity of seeking wisdom. Does it develop overnight? Sometimes. But soul-searing wisdom requires the experience of seeking it and then holding on to it once you get it, that is, remember. We all have opportunities to call upon Wisdom, and to willfully ignore or forget it. Many of life's wounds are caused by those choices, like something hurtful we said and then regretted. Thankfully, God uses those same wounds and regrets to grow our wisdom for the next time. Then, we don't think twice. It sure feels nice when we use it.

Seeking results in focus. Once a baby is born, parents immediately cross over from planning and dreaming into daily caring for an infant, which brings a steep learning curve and many unknowns. In the consuming whirlwind of becoming a parent, it's easy to put spiritual life on autopilot.

In autopilot mode, we let events and ideas carry us where they will. Meanwhile, we often tend to be hyperfocused on other areas, which sometimes are more important and sometimes aren't. In 1972, an airplane crashed into the Florida everglades because the pilot and co-pilot were hyper focused on a landing gear indicator light that had burned out. They didn't notice that the autopilot had been accidently disengaged and the plane lost altitude.

Even with the demands of a newborn, you won't have a problem focusing on God if you are continually seeking him. During feeding, strolling, rocking, changing, cleaning, and resting, God will be more present to you when you look for him. You sense his response and know his nearness. You then see his work, even in the busyness of family life. When disaster strikes, you will be exactly where you need to be:

> *The Lord is a refuge for the oppressed,*
> *a stronghold in times of trouble.*
> *Those who know your name trust in you,*
> *for you, Lord, have never forsaken those who seek you.*
> —PSALM 9:9-10

Applying It in Parenting and Family Life

As your seeking keeps your spiritual journey alive, you discover it has as much individuality and creativity as the physical side of your life. You see the influence of seeking and its silent partnership with all that is visible. Let's examine a few everyday ways that seeking can influence your relationships with God and family. In the following sections, you will:

- **Practice God's presence.** Resist the tendency to be preoccupied and instead enjoy being with God.
- **Cultivate beneficial patterns.** Become a creature of spiritual habit with routines that also healthfully impact your child.
- **Pursue fruitful knowledge.** Open your heart and mind to spiritual truths to guide you on the bumpy road of family life.

Do not be discouraged if you have lost the desire to seek or have never had it. Remember, God is the initiator. An easy first step in seeking God is simply to pray for the desire to seek.

1. Practice God's presence

As the deer pants for streams of water, so my soul pants for you, my God. My soul thirsts for God, for the living God. When can I go and meet with God?

—Psalm 42:1-2

> A mind surrendered to and focused on God is seeking God's will for every action. And all the time, we are being slowly conformed to his likeness, becoming who he made us to be, according to his specific plan for our lives.

In the physical realm, being with a person nonstop can be rather taxing. We love our spouse and kids, but we really don't want to spend every moment with them. We need a break, a little absence to make the heart grow fonder. Brief separation can give perspective. We are usually thankful to be back together.

But in the spiritual realm, separation makes us flounder. We falsely think we can get on without God for much of the day. In God's absence, a soul will pant for the thing it can't name or own or control. Have you ever just wanted a break from a constant inner nagging, a break from *yourself*? Our selves are surely the most exhausting company we keep.

When a life is dedicated to God and seeking him, that unnamed spiritual thirst finds a wellspring. We find peace from that unrest we so often inflict on ourselves.

The desperate plea of the psalmist quoted above was answered when Jesus died on the Cross and the 60-foot veil that shielded God's presence in the Holy of Holies was ripped open from the top, down (Matthew 27:51). Sin, which for so long created a barrier between God and man, was vanquished.

No longer would God's presence be exclusive to the high priest only on the Day of Atonement. There would be no more need for animal sacrifice because the perfect Lamb forever changed God's account of our sin (Hebrews 6:20). We would no longer die if we encountered God in his full blinding glory and holiness because we have Jesus, fully God and fully man, as our Mediator (1 Timothy 2:5). But even more than that: Our God with us, Emmanuel, became accessible as God within us.

After he returned to the Father, and was seated at his right hand, Jesus sent believers an Advocate to help them, the Holy Spirit. The Spirit lives in the core of believers, guiding their days on earth until they see Jesus face to face. With millions and millions of holy temples of God's presence throughout the world and throughout time, God's love has infiltrated humankind and powered it to achieve even more than Jesus did while here, just as he predicted (John 14:12).

For the Christian life, the willful focus on God's presence is our day in, day out spiritual nourishment. We don't need to do anything, but turn our minds to God and be with him. Farmers can do this. Business leaders can do this. Students and children can do this, too. The cost is free. And it can be done anywhere, anyplace, anytime. No special degrees or certification are needed. No one is rejected, no one, including moms and dads overwhelmed by newborns.

But there's even more. Although God's creation has magnificent predictability and reliability, it also has infinite variety. The greatest beauty of God's interaction with an individual is that he tailor-makes it for that individual. This is where your ability to seek can reap you the highly customized fit God has just for you and your purpose (Psalm 139).

"Your place in Heaven will seem to be made for you and you alone, because you were made for it—made for it stitch by stitch as a glove is made for a hand," C. S. Lewis writes.[3] Jesus announced that this Heaven is near (Mark 1:15). It is here and now. Anyone who has experienced God personally knows that this is true. Doesn't that excite and intrigue us all the more?

To encourage our journeys, we can look to our common spiritual roots, and the experiences of believers throughout time. We will mention just a few here.

"The fact that we are made in God's image shows us how great are the dignity and loveliness of the soul," wrote Saint Teresa of Avila in the 1500s.[4] She describes an interior castle, "where God and the soul have their most secret conversations.... If we reflect on this, we will see that the soul of a just man is a garden in which the Beloved takes great delight. What do you imagine that dwelling must be like for God to delight in it?"[5]

Another well-known practitioner of God's presence was 17th century French monk Brother Lawrence. Driven by his love for God, "that till death I shall have done all that is in me to love him,"[6] Brother Lawrence could glide above the most tiring circumstances in daily life.

> The time of business does not differ from the time of prayer, and in the noise and clatter of my kitchen, while several persons are at the same time calling for different things, I possess God in as great tranquility as if I were upon my knees at the blessed sacrament.[7]

In the early 1900s, missionary Frank Laubach developed a similar habit of drawing closer to God. The founder of a world-wide literacy organization, Laubach would say a small prayer for everyone he encountered, actively think of God in all that he did, and constantly seek God's will before he would even move a hand. Laubach wrote about his experiences and created a guide for what he called the Game of Minutes, which is so basic that even a child could do it:

> The simple practice requires only a gentle pressure of the will, not more than a person can exert easily. It grows easier as the habit becomes fixed. Yet it transforms life into Heaven.

Everybody takes on a new richness, and all the world seems tinted with glory.[8]

Laubach described his growing intimacy with God as "a great sense of the close-up, warm, heart of reality. God simply creeps in and you know he is here in your heart. He has become your friend by working along with you." Though he served in distant, unusual lands for a long time, Laubach said he felt a keen familiarity in God's "homey" universe.[9]

Just like any relationship, it takes time to build intimacy with God, so don't give up if you falter. Many husbands and wives are blindsided when the busyness of parenting hits, and they no longer have their quiet time. In that season, a steady stream of shorter prayers and memorized Scripture will be your lifelines for staying connected to God's voice, just like Brother Lawrence in his clamoring kitchen.

> "And surely I am with you always, to the very end of the age."
> —Matthew 28:20

In God's presence, we find rest from the incessant goading of our fitful selves (Matthew 11:28). Such a mind focused on God is steadily surrendering and seeking his will. We actually hear from him in unmistakable ways through Scripture, or a loud inner voice not of us, or through circumstances, or the words of other believers. And all the time, we are being gradually conformed to his likeness, the unique souls he made us to be.

There is great promise for a new marriage and a new family with this kind of life. It means freedom from religious obligations and instead devotion to God, who will faithfully guide you. And if you honestly assess and focus on your own spiritual affairs with God, you then will be less likely to criticize others (Matthew 7:3).

What would it look like for you to practice the presence of God in the presence of those you love? As a dad? As a mom? It will have the same effect that Jesus had. Your loved ones will be drawn to what they see of him in you. In the meantime, the yearning—the applying of your will to quench your thirst for God by being in his presence—will be its own reward.

Build & Grow

Learn

- In Psalm 42:1-2, the psalmist passionately identifies his need as spiritual thirst. Look in the Bible for other references to thirsting for God. How "thirsty" are you? What propels your desire to go and meet with God?

Absorb

- Prepare now for the change to come in your routine after your baby arrives. Memorize Bible verses that will later comfort you with God's steady presence and help you to seek his will, for example:

"Come to me, all you who are weary and burdened, and I will give you rest. Take my yoke upon you and learn from me, for I am gentle and humble in heart, and you will find rest for your souls. For my yoke is easy and my burden is light" (Matthew 11:28-30).

"As a mother comforts her child, so will I comfort you" (Isaiah 66:13).

"For we do not have a high priest who is unable to empathize with our weaknesses, but we have one who has been tempted in every way, just as we are—yet he did not sin. Let us then approach God's throne of grace with confidence, so that we may receive mercy and find grace to help us in our time of need" (Hebrews 4:15-16).

"He gives strength to the weary and increases the power of the weak" (Isaiah 40:29).

"But those who hope in the Lord will renew their strength. They will soar on wings like eagles; they will run and not grow weary, they will walk and not be faint" (Isaiah 40:31).

Praise

- Let it sink in that God *wants to be with you.* Isn't that amazing?

Connect

- Tell your spouse or small group about the most recent time your prayerful seeking resulted in a customized response from God, and how you knew it was just for you. Everyone will be encouraged.

2. Cultivate beneficial patterns

His divine power has given us everything we need for a godly life through our knowledge of him who called us by his own glory and goodness.
—2 PETER 1:3

> Reflexes and routines can either build your personal and family life with God or impede it. Beneficial patterns train us to cooperate with the Spirit.

One of the biggest adjustments for newlyweds is learning to co-exist with each other's unexpected and sometimes annoying habits. Even minor things, like the direction the toilet paper rolls off or the way toothpaste globs on the tube, can become major sticking points throughout a marriage.

We are creatures of habit. The habits in our lives become second nature and construct patterns for our way in the world. When you become a parent, you witness in real time how your child develops habits as quickly and reflexively as that first suck of a thumb. Habits can very easily take root, but prove almost impossible to weed out because, for better or worse, something about them work for us.

What is true about habits in our physical life is also true about habits in our spiritual life. Established habits seem to have an overwhelming advantage over our best intentions and willpower. How many New

Year's resolutions putter out after the first few weeks? How many new gimmicks will we try in order to break a bad habit or establish a good one? How often do we put off going to church because we just can't seem to get into the swing of it?

We all possess the stain of creatures fallen from our original design, and rather than submitting to God's good will we live under the tumult of our own. Anyone who has exerted their willpower in strenuous effort and then failed understands how utterly weak the human will can be. That's what Paul refers to as our wretched bodies being at war with our best intentions (Romans 7:24).

Happily, we have a Deliverer who intends, if we will permit him, to restore us as sons and daughters who can dwell in the presence of our Father God. We desperately need Jesus' help. We are living, breathing, walking, talking contradictions who cannot cultivate beneficial patterns in our lives until he frees and empowers us to do so from our core. "The strongest human will is always the one that is surrendered to God's will and acts with it," Dallas Willard writes, as the meaning of Paul's statement "It is no longer I who live, but Christ who lives in me" (Galatians 2:20, ESV).[10]

What would surrendering to God's will and establishing "Christ in me" look like in your daily life?

You could set the alarm 30 minutes earlier in the morning. The beep that wakes you up is your cue to pray before you get out of bed. Memorize and daily repeat passages like Psalm 143:8-10 to give your day perspective. Shuffle to the kitchen for coffee, and then curl up in a chair with the Bible. Meet with God. That would be a great pattern! Over time, you'll find you can't live without such spiritually nourishing habits. You'll notice more resilience in the tough times. Your spouse and child will notice and be influenced by you in their own ways.

Throughout your day, rather than your usual internal mutterings or mental playbacks, address your thoughts to God, as an ongoing silent conversation. "Lord, this line at the grocery store is long. I sure am thankful for everything in this basket, though. Who would you have me bring to mind for prayer while I wait?" You'll be surprised at how God uses you to bring love into a hurting world.

Perhaps evening is the time beneficial patterns are needed most. You've had a full day at work and home. You have many wonderful distractions at hand to give your thoughts and emotions a break. At this point, you just want to tune out. There's nothing wrong with that. But be careful that what you do is good for you and your relationship with those around you. Go to bed at the same time with your spouse and pray together before you turn out the light. Such simple habits will build a sense of togetherness that can withstand the harder days.

These are just some of the ways to cooperate with the Spirit, who is after all, doing the heavy lifting here, not us. Even Jesus established beneficial patterns to revive his soul: "…crowds of people came to hear him and to be healed of their sicknesses. But Jesus often withdrew to lonely places and prayed" (Luke 5:15-16).

Build & Grow

Learn

- *"…crowds of people came to hear him and to be healed of their sicknesses. But Jesus often withdrew to lonely places and prayed" (Luke 5:15-16).* Why do you think this was a beneficial pattern for Jesus?

Absorb

- We are living, breathing, walking, talking contradictions who cannot cultivate beneficial patterns in our lives until God frees us and empowers us. Happily, we have a Deliverer who desires to do so. Is there a routine that ensnares you? Is there something you need God's power to start?

Praise

- Shift your mental energy from focusing on irritations and fears to recognizing God in everyday life and seeking his will. Ask, "What do you want to teach me right now?" Pray short prayers instead of trying to solve problems alone. Observe what seeking God's will does for you.

Connect

- Think about your morning routine and discretionary time in the evenings. Identify alone time to invest in your faith. What else builds togetherness and unity in your marriage and family? Establishing beneficial patterns now, makes them easier to continue after the baby arrives. Give appreciation to your spouse along the way for helping you stay on track with good habits.

3. Pursue fruitful knowledge

Hold on to instruction, do not let it go; guard it well, for it is your life.
—Proverbs 4:13

> The Word of God is active and alive. Open your Bible
> to encounter a Person, and experience the benefits
> of his life-giving wisdom.

As you marry and start a family, you go into an active fact-gathering mode. You research, subscribe to news, read books, talk with experienced friends and mentors—all of this is seeking. Your instincts are spot on! You realize how much you don't know. You have an appetite for new knowledge. The only way to be the spouse or parent you want to be is to seek and grow in those roles.

Hunger for knowledge, the need to know, has been a foundation for spiritual development throughout time. On the spiritual journey, that hunger is fed by God's Word, his history with humankind as recorded in the Bible. "For the word of God is alive and active. Sharper than any double-edged sword, it penetrates even to dividing soul and spirit, joints and marrow; it judges the thoughts and attitudes of the heart" (Hebrews 4:12).

Rather than studying the Bible to absorb facts about God, consider it more like immersing into the mind of the Person you would like to know. The Holy Bible—written in three languages over the course of 1,500 years by more than 40 authors from as many generations and every walk of life, in places as varied as deserts, cities, palaces, prisons, caves, and huts—is truly a miracle you can hold in your hands.[11] The consistency of God and humankind's reaction to him amidst such vastly different circumstances is striking. We can thank God that he chose and trained a people committed to writing, learning, and preserving our Scripture.

The beauty of pursuing knowledge of God in the Bible, its fruits and reward, is that even something previously known, like the account of Noah's ark or our Lord's Sermon on the Mount, can be held in a new light and offer fresh insights not previously possible. The delight of discovery, making profound new connections, will inspire you to hunger for still more.

Reading and re-reading the entire Bible in a continuous, even methodical fashion is a good way to get grounded in it. This would be one of your most fruit-yielding beneficial patterns. Get a Study Bible version and make notes in it. Use one of the many "read the Bible in a year" plans and devote time to completing it. Don't worry if it takes you two years, or if you fall asleep sometimes or find the text uninteresting. Just commit yourself to hearing from God from start to finish. Your knowledge and wisdom will accumulate. You'll have more capacity to digest and reflect on writings that before escaped your notice. You'll perceive internal connections in God's plan and relate their meaning to your day. You'll actually *enjoy* this new life-affirming window on God, just as he delights in you.

Some people prefer to walk through the Bible systematically in their private time and then join a Bible study class to go deeper into a book or subject in it. Reading from Psalms, "the book of the soul," with your spouse each night is an impactful way to be reminded of the spiritual ups and downs everyone faces, and to meditate on God's promises and his faithfulness.

Another popular method, the Discovery Bible Study, excludes outside sources or interpretations in order to illuminate the text in deeply personal ways, using the same discussion questions for each reading.

Your growing knowledge about God will create a filter for everything you encounter, and you will be positively transformed along the way "by the renewing of your mind. Then you will be able to test and approve what God's will is—his good, pleasing, and perfect will" (Romans 12:2). Engaging with God's word results in a dynamic, interactive conversation with him that permeates a soul, a marriage, and the whole of family life.

Build & Grow

Learn

- Look closely at what the Bible teaches about the Bible. Look up Hebrews 4:12 and 2 Timothy 3:16-17, and write them down. Considering both of these references, what would applying Scripture look like in your own circumstances?

Absorb

- Reading and re-reading the entire Bible in a continuous, even methodical fashion is a good way to get grounded in it. Do you or your spouse read the Bible now? How could your marriage and family life benefit if you study the Bible on a regular basis together?

Praise

- Reading the Bible grows your knowledge about God and thus helps you recognize him in the little details of your day. You'll actually *enjoy* this new life-affirming window on God, and you will be positively transformed along the way. Jot down something transformational that you learned from Scripture recently.

Connect

- The Bible is meant to be experienced both personally and in community. Ask other couples, or members of your family, or a few friends to start a "read the Bible in a year" plan with you, even if you all have already done it. Together, you could commit to studying and memorizing a passage in the Bible that is especially relevant now, like Psalm 139 referred to several times in this book. In this season of your life, even memorizing one meaningful and rich verse for the year can be of great value in many circumstances.

Plan Ahead

Choose points about SEEK to carry with you:

1.

2.

3.

Organize a SEEK gift for your child:

Designate a central place in your home such as the kitchen or family room for a chalk or bulletin board to display Scripture verses. Pick passages together that remind you who God is and who you are in him, individually and as a family. Also, write down prayers and praises to God. Update your writings as you and your child move through different seasons of learning. As you seek him together, you will gain wisdom and encouragement for your unique paths.

SEEK early childhood board book connections:
Jesus Saves Me and *Mud Puddle Hunting Day*

Question

Questioning is the ability you have to spur and guide your life's growth, and a hallmark practice of earnest discipleship under Jesus. The same process plays itself over in marriage and parenting, and it is indispensable to your child's developing spiritual life.

Newborn Fact of Life

 Your child will ask you about God.
Your personal experiences will help you answer.

God gives children a remarkable curiosity, doesn't he? It's the engine that powers their brains with new information, fueling a hunger to know and grow. Babies examine objects with their hands and mouths until they are old enough to walk and talk. Toddlers are famously inquisitive with their *Hows* and *Whys*.

A curious child is your chance to give the budding new soul a true picture of God. Young children usually tune out a lecture or sermon. It's too much information and the timing isn't right for them to receive it. But when children ask questions, their hearts and minds roll out the welcome mat for what you have to say. And they want the answers short and straight. You can thank God for that!

Once children are out of the toddler years and experience more of the push and pull of the world, they will ask you about matters troubling them. You might be surprised by their depth. Their questions grow in complexity from "Where does God live?" to "Will I go to Hell because I told a lie?"

Pre-teens and teens often ask about the technical, apologetic aspects of faith to either prove or disprove what they've learned. They'll typically invite more of a discussion or debate. But young children go for the spiritual jugular, often from out of the blue: Why did grandma have to die? Will ever I see her again?

Such questions are golden moments, the opportunity to aggressively push back on the world's erroneous depictions of God and Heaven. The question is, are you ready to answer? The trustworthy Bible says yes, because you have a personal relationship with God and have lived through experiences with him that inform you.

The heart of God's desire for parenting lies in Deuteronomy 6. It's also here and in Exodus that Scripture assures you that your child will question you about the reasons for your faith, and God instructs you how to answer. After teaching the commandments, Moses exhorts parents to hold them on their own hearts and then, "Impress them on your children" (Deuteronomy 6:6).

Parents are to hand down God's commands through their words and actions during the routines of daily life: "Talk about them when you sit at home and when you walk along the road, when you lie down and when you get up. Tie them as symbols on your hands and bind them on your foreheads. Write them on the doorframes of your houses and on your gates" (Deuteronomy 6:7-9). A parent's life with God will be evident.

And then, "In the future, when your son asks you, 'What is the meaning of the stipulations, decrees, and laws the Lord our God has commanded you?' tell him…" (Deuteronomy 6:20). The emphasis here is on a maturing curiosity a child will have about the parents' faith.

Scripture demonstrates a similar pattern with questions from growing children about Passover and first-born consecration (Exodus 12:26, 13:14). God instructs parents to answer with a personal account of his mighty acts for them: "On that day tell your son, 'I do this because of what the Lord did for me when I came out of Egypt'" (Exodus 13:8). In each passage, the question-provoking occasions involve miraculous milestones in God's history with his people. The events reminded people who God is and what life with him means.

At this moment, you have the same kind of miraculous milestones, and they will help you answer your child. Like the Israelite parents, you've had a journey with God to the Promised Land. The people of Moses' time had their miraculous deliverance from Egypt and were kept alive by manna in the desert. Today, you have the miraculous saving act of Jesus Christ, your Bread of Life. You love and honor God because of who he is and what he has done in your life. We all have an experience to which we can point and say, "Only God can do that!" Or better yet, "My God did that for me."

> "Curiosity is the thirst of the soul."
> —Samuel Johnson

Pray that your child asks you questions about God. Pray that you answer in just the way your child needs to hear. Pray *with* your child for God to send you answers when you don't have them. Sometimes there will be no answer for you to give. God's ways are not our ways (Isaiah 55:8). Help your child sit with unanswerable questions, the ambiguities in faith, by trusting in God's goodness together. Clinging to God's unchanging ways helps us when we don't understand life's challenges (Romans 8:28).

You've already got a strong start. God chose you to teach and nurture the soul he made. You're searching and learning from God in planning for your important new role. You will know and love your child better than anyone except God. And if God is for you, and for your child, who can be against you?

What Questioning Can Do in Marriage & Family

With all wisdom and understanding, he made known to us the mystery of his will according to his good pleasure, which he purposed in Christ, to be put into effect when the times reach their fulfillment—to bring unity to all things in heaven and on earth under Christ.

—EPHESIANS 1:8-10

Entering a new phase in life is exciting, but it can be stressful with all the decisions you face. Which career path would be best? Should I move to a new city? When will I be ready to settle down? Is this person the one? Do I want children?

The answers are not so clear-cut, yet they chart the direction of your life. What else will I miss if I take this path? What if I make a terribly wrong choice? What is God's will for me?

Questioning who you want to be is a valuable exercise, a mechanism of sorts for eventually becoming that person. It is a healthy lifelong activity if it doesn't devolve into navel gazing, or an excessive contemplation of oneself. Questioning leads to answers that call for action and result in change. *To question* is the ability you have to spur and guide your life's growth. The same process plays itself over in your new marriage and parenting life.

Whereas seeking involves pursuing intimacy with God, questioning examines your thoughts about him, your understanding of faith, and points to what you need to discover and know. It serves as an essential part of your spiritual growth throughout your life, and it is indispensible to your child's developing spiritual life.

Planning for your child is likely to evoke some deeply spiritual questions within your own heart. How will God help me in this new stage of life? How can I be sure my child will believe in him? Is my faith healthy and ready to start leading the way for my child? How will I know?

Though neglected or discouraged in some religious circles, questioning is actually an important instrument for discovering truth— God's truth about who you are and your circumstances, and truth about God and your relationship with him. No church or spiritual mentor or book like this can find it for you. You have an intensely personal task at hand.

"When truth is discovered by someone else, it loses something of its attractiveness," wrote Russian novelist Aleksandr Solzhenitsyn, who was under Soviet oppression.[1] Doesn't his statement ring true for the spiritual life? We do not like to be force-fed or deprived.

Another novelist, who chronicled the free-wheeling American frontier, observed, "Truth is stranger than Fiction, but it is because Fiction is obliged to stick to possibilities; Truth isn't."[2] How funny and true Mark Twain's words are! The adventure of a life illuminated by *God's* truth will prove that anything is possible and nothing is unbelievable.

In our culture, we have heard about the Nativity and Resurrection so much that we don't fully appreciate how astounding these events truly were. They were even new experiences for God.[3] As part of his mission, Jesus taught aspects of God's plan that were dramatically new to everyone. No one expected what he revealed. "The people were all so amazed that they asked each other, 'What is this? A new teaching—and with authority!'" (Mark 1:27).

Jesus' words upended people's take on reality about God and inspired violent reactions. His teaching was—and still is—against the grain of the times, above and beyond all that had ever been considered about ethics and morals and God. Scottish Theologian Thomas F. Torrance writes:

> It is as such that revelation proceeds from God to man, breaking sovereignly into human life and thought, calling into question what people claim to know, and directing their thinking beyond themselves altogether.... For the radically new conception of God proclaimed in the Gospel calls for a complete transformation of man's outlook in terms of a new divine order, which cannot be derived from or inferred from anything conceived by man before.[4]

Wouldn't it be odd if we had no questions at all for God?

Questioning is a hallmark practice of earnest discipleship under Jesus. In his time on earth, Jesus demonstrated great patience with his disciples, who struggled in their understanding of his revelations, even after living several years in his physical presence. They asked, "What does he mean by 'a little while'? We don't understand what he is saying" (John 16:18). You can almost hear their minds explode!

Jesus never insisted they stop asking questions—far from it. He said, "Ask and it will be given to you; seek and you will find; knock and the door will be opened to you" (Matthew 7:7). He also questioned them in order to spur their thinking: "Who do you say I am?" (Matthew 16:15). "You do not want to leave too, do you?" (John 6:7).

His harshest words were not for those who were struggling to understand, but for those who refused to even try. Jesus said, "This is the verdict: Light has come into the world, but people loved darkness instead of light because their deeds were evil" (John 3:20).

Jesus' method of teaching is not unlike the way you will teach your own children. Your child's spontaneous asking of questions will result in fruitful exchanges that drive truths home. Such questions are golden moments—open invitations for you to share, not lecture, jewels of knowledge and wisdom with a willing heart.

For a grownup's part, questioning must also display the endearing features of a child that Jesus so desires. A questioning heart is an open, impressionable heart. The questioner asks with humility, harbors no ulterior motives, and sincerely hopes for a helpful answer that will then be put into use.

"One is apt to admire the beautiful sentiment, and to forget that children were more to Jesus than helpless, gentle creatures to be loved and protected. They were his chief parable of the Kingdom of Heaven," John Watson writes in *The Mind of The Master*. For Jesus, a child illustrates the ideal qualities of Christian character, because a child "does not assert nor aggrandize himself. Because he has no memory for injuries and no room in his heart for a grudge. Because he has no previous opinions, and is not ashamed to confess his ignorance." A child has an imagination and is willing to use it to live "amid things unseen and eternal."[5]

God's view of children is great news for adult believers. Becoming like a child means we receive the gift of a fresh start with freedom in God's family. Can you physically get your purity back for the blessing of your current marriage? No, but you can spiritually, because as we've learned, each day God's mercies are new (Lamentations 3:22-23). We put off the old and take on the new, reminding ourselves we are a new creation, born of the Spirit (John 3, Ephesians 4).

As children of God, we also must realize our vulnerability and test everything so that we may avoid evil, and hold on to the good (1 Thessalonians 5:21). This world has another ruler, for a time, whom Jesus emphatically calls a liar: "He was a murderer from the beginning, and does not stand in the truth, because there is no truth in him. When he lies, he speaks out of his own character, for he is a liar and the father of lies" (John 8:44, ESV).

At the outset of his ministry, Jesus announced the arrival of God's kingdom advancing in this world and bringing a whole new opportunity to be part of it (Mark 1:15). When he returned to the Father, Jesus kept his promise to send a Helper, available to all who would believe. "All this I have spoken while still with you. But the Counselor, the Holy Spirit, whom the Father will send in my name, will teach you all things and will remind you of everything I have said to you" (John

14:25-26). The Holy Spirit, at your core, is the source of many of your questions, and likewise will lead you to the answers.

Be devoted to fueling your curiosity, a great power of the mind that aids your seeking. If you don't desire to read Scripture or have burning questions about life in the spirit, if your physical life is too over-loaded to even allow space for curiosity, then ask God to give it to you. And give yourself a little mental breathing room.

There is only one truth, God's truth, but it has unlimited ways of resounding within and impacting an individual's soul. We are inspired by the testimonies and experiences that others have with God, but ours will be different, and so we must find meaning in them for our-selves in our circumstances through questioning. Let's look at just a few ways questioning will guide your journey:

Questioning sheds light on traps. In our everyday lives we con-tinually encounter traps of worldly patterns and expectations with-in social settings, at the office, in playgroups, even at church. Paul warns, "See to it that no one takes you captive through hollow and deceptive philosophy, which depends on human tradition and the elemental spiritual forces of this world rather than on Christ" (Colossians 2:8).

Just examining why you are thinking what you are thinking is enough to realize that it might be for the wrong reasons. Newlyweds and new parents can easily find themselves in the comparison trap, for example. Someone else always has a better job or smarter kids. Couples at church seem to have it all together. Why are you feeling so down on yourself?

When you recognize the pangs of comparison for what they are, remember Paul's words: "Each one should test their own actions. Then they can take pride in themselves alone, without comparing them-selves to someone else, for each one should carry their own load" (Galatians 6:3-5). You can't do that if you are always looking over your shoulder.

Worldly traps like comparison and competition—always trying to one-up one another—lead to jealousy, covetousness, malice, lies, and more. Ask God to make plain these enemies of the spirit and to help you resist the world's pressure. His Spirit will raise flags for you to question why you do what you do and lead you from such unhealthy traps.

Questioning sheds light on motives. Some earnest religious leaders of Jesus' time asked him sincere questions with a searching heart. From one such exchange between Jesus and Nicodemus recorded in John 3, we get the most profound statement in the Bible about God's plan (verse 16). It is the basis for the title of this book. Take time to read and re-read that fascinating, revealing chapter.

Other religious leaders, however, asked Jesus questions to trap, test, or embarrass him. *Who did this man from Galilee think he was?* Jesus sometimes responded to those ploys with questions of his own, which exposed their motives and silenced them. He asked them:

- "Whose portrait is this? And whose inscription?" (Mark 12:16)

- "What is written in the Law? How do you read it?" (Luke 10:26)

- "How can the guests of the bridegroom mourn while he is with them?" (Matthew 9:15)

- "And why do you break the command of God for the sake of your tradition?" (Matthew 15:3)

- "Why are you thinking these things in your hearts? Which is easier: to say, 'Your sins are forgiven,' or to say, 'Get up and walk'?" (Luke 5:22)

God's enemy is skilled at questioning *us* about God and insinuating a better way. "Did God really say, 'You must not eat from any tree in the garden'?" (Genesis 3:1). Don't let those questions mislead you. We must question the origin of the thoughts that pop into our minds. We are bombarded with such worldly insinuations every day in advertising and media. Dishonest words, selfish claims, and vain images have the power to distort our inner lives unless we filter them with questions that literally fight back with truth. We need the Lord's help in discerning the difference between truth and untruth. Like King David in Psalm 139:23-24, we can pray:

Search me, O God, and know my heart;
test me and know my anxious thoughts.

See if there is any offensive way in me,
  And lead me in the way everlasting.
                    —Psalm 139:23-24

Use Jesus' method of questioning to expose motives—yours and those of others. And as with Nicodemus, Jesus will reveal hidden things to you.

Questioning sheds light on assumptions. Christians often operate under assumptions about God and faith that are just not true, though they might seem true on the surface. Have you heard any of these?

—*If you worry, that means you don't trust God.*

—*When prayers for healing go unanswered, it is because the person suffering lacks faith.*

—*As God's authority on earth, an ordained minister must be fully trusted and followed, no questions asked.*

—*God will never make us go through more than we can bear.*

—*When we get to Heaven, we will be singing all the time forever.*

The list of false assumptions could go on and on.

Most of us have experiences of discovering wrongful thinking after years of following Christ. God's people have been this way from the start. The oldest book in the Bible, Job is a lengthy chronicle of false assumptions among friends about God.

Jesus came to earth during a religiously oppressive era that layered wrongful thinking upon wrongful thinking about God through a morass of traditions and laws. How refreshing his words must have been: "So Jesus said to the Jews who had believed him, 'If you abide in my word, you are truly my disciples, and you will know the truth, and the truth will set you free'" (John 8:31-32, ESV). Disciples ask questions in order to correct misguided assumptions.

Applying It in Marriage and Family Life

Getting married and having children present the two greatest opportunities and the greatest challenges for your relationship with God.

Confidently exercise your ability *to question* in these helpful ways:

- **Grapple with God**. Events in marriage and family lead us to question God's attributes, plans, and actions.

- **Recognize the enemy.** As primarily spiritual beings, we must recognize our role in the epic spiritual battle of all time.

- **Tether to truth.** Time and again God's truth reigns and will prevail until his plans are fulfilled for a new Heaven and Earth.

Far from being a sign of hard-heartedness or unbelief, questions about faith and God are the sign of a seeking heart to make meaning out of life experiences and draw nearer to God. A questioning faith will be a robust, thriving faith that can begin in the earliest days of childhood.

1. Grapple with God

Whom have I in heaven but you?
  And earth has nothing I desire besides you.
My flesh and my heart may fail,
  But God is the strength of my heart
  and my portion forever.
                                    —PSALM 73:25-26

On the road to becoming more like Christ, God necessarily leads us through times that inspire questioning. In love, he shows us meaning in our frustrations, loss, and suffering.

As believers we sometimes think, "When I get to Heaven, I'm going to ask God about (fill in the blank)." We have a huge list for God, don't we? For one thing, why does he allow the miscarriage of a new life that had been so long prayed for and rejoiced over with praises to him? Why can't some godly couples conceive while others who aren't even wanting children easily get pregnant?

We question God's plans—the paradoxes, enigmas, and traumas involved with them. Can Pharaoh be blamed when it was God who hardened his heart? Why did God order his chosen people to wage brutal battles against others? How could he allow Jesus to be so horribly betrayed and tortured? Why did he allow abuse to happen to me?

Nonbelievers ask such questions of God, too. The real paradox is that apart from God, questioning is an exercise in futility, as the book of Ecclesiastes so well illustrates. "I have seen all the things that are done under the sun; all of them are meaningless, a chasing after the wind" (1:14). Only God's true perspective gives our lives meaning.

And so we must grapple with our questions *with God*, in order to be enlightened and to have our misperceptions about him clarified or corrected. What we believe about him defines our lives and the philosophies by which we operate.

"It is impossible to keep our moral practices sound and our inward attitudes right while our idea of God is erroneous or inadequate," A.W. Tozer writes. "If we would bring back spiritual power to our lives, we must begin to think of God more nearly as he is."[6]

In the process, we must be careful that our grappling is not judgmental of God or others, that we approach him through prayer and study with open-eyed awareness of our station in this life and the natural condition of our own hearts.

But we are not left to our own devices. God gives us such illuminating writings as the books of Job, Ecclesiastes, and Psalms, with insights into the mysteries surrounding God's purposes and the reality of his divine attributes. These books of the Bible teach us how to reverentially wrestle with God in order to live out the faith he gives us.

One of the most difficult aspects of going through tough times—a miscarriage, a terrible job, an unfaithful spouse, an incurable disease—is understanding God's purpose in letting it happen. A common reaction is to believe that God has abandoned or turned against us or that we have done something wrong to displease him. We feel awfully alone, crushed.

Here, we will turn to our spiritual forefather, Job. His experience is foundational in understanding human history with God. We witness the horror of God permitting a good man's undoing. He lost his wealth, children, home, status, and then finally, his health. Covered in sores from head to toe, Job cried out, "What I feared has come upon me; what I dreaded has happened to me. I have no peace, no quietness; I have no rest, but only turmoil" (3:25-26). Even still, he held onto his faith and refused to curse God and end his life, as his wife urged him to do.

As readers, we are privy to a prior discussion between God and Satan, whom we are told roams the earth scouting for souls. God himself suggested Job as one whose faith was unshakeable, and God permits Satan's advancing campaign against Job. His greatest grief was yet to come. "Now Satan proceeds to assault the innermost stronghold of Job's being: his spirit. The human spirit is, after all, the ultimate reality of a human life," Ray C. Stedman observes.[7] To be sure: "The human spirit can endure in sickness, but a crushed spirit who can bear?" (Proverbs 18:14).

For the next 35 chapters, we witness intense questioning among Job and his three visiting friends, who alternately accuse him of a shallow faith or hidden evil, much as Satan had, but they never simply pray with him. Job comes dangerously close to accusing God as his enemy. Had not Job been good in every way? Only a fifth person, younger Elihu, who speaks up toward the end, rightly views Job's experience with an understanding of God's humbling sovereignty. Elihu's words, recorded in Chapter 37, are a masterpiece of praise for God.

Now the group hears from God himself, who addresses Job directly, not his friends: "Who is this that darkens my counsel with words without knowledge? Brace yourself like a man; I will question you, and you shall answer me" (38:2-3). Oh, boy. God's 70 questions have painfully obvious answers for Job. You will have to read this for yourself. It is the longest quotation of God in the Bible.

The biggest pitfall in faith—in life—is buying the lie that we are here to have a good time and be happy, that if we are good enough God owes us prosperity. Yet nothing in the human experience supports that operating assumption. Nothing in creation does. This life is unquestionably difficult, no matter who you are, what your circumstances, or how many plans you make otherwise. The greater question is: why is that true? Again, none of this makes sense apart from God. The apostle Paul explains:

I consider that our present sufferings are not worth comparing with the glory that will be revealed in us. For the creation waits in eager expectation for the children of God to be revealed. For the creation was subjected to frustration, not by its own choice, but by the will of the one who subjected it, in hope that the creation itself will be liberated from its bondage to decay and brought into the freedom and glory of the children of God.

We know that the whole creation has been groaning as in the pains of childbirth right up to the present time. No only so, but we ourselves, who have the first fruits of the Spirit, groan inwardly as we wait eagerly for our adoption to sonship, the redemption of our bodies. For in this hope we were saved (Romans 8:18-24).

On this road to becoming more like Christ, God necessarily leads us through times that inspire questioning. Here, he actively engages with us. In a spirit of love, we ask him to give us his perspective. In love, he shows us meaning in our frustrations, loss, and suffering. This is how we have joy in suffering, because we have meaning. And we have God. As an exercise of faith, Job's purposeful questioning—and yours—leads to a greater understanding of who God is. This was the saving grace for Job who said in the end:

I know that you can do all things; no plan of yours can be thwarted. You asked, 'Who is this that obscures my counsel without knowledge?' Surely I spoke of things I did not understand, things too wonderful for me to know. You said, 'Listen now, and I will speak; I will question you, and you shall answer me.' My ears had heard of you but now my eyes have seen you (Job 42:2-5).

Deep breaks through to deep and touches the chords of the soul. It is amazing to be caught up in the divine flow of God's purpose and love.

Build & Grow

Learn

- God answers Job's questions with questions. Read Job 38-42 and list the attributes of God that stand out to you. Consider which of these can help you in the midst of your own circumstances now.

Absorb

- It is amazing to be caught up in the divine flow of God's purpose. In a spirit of love, we ask him to give us his perspective. In love, he shows us meaning in our frustrations, loss, and suffering. With this hope of divine purpose in mind, ask God one hard spiritual question.

Praise

- Why do you think God's questions—though powerful, strong, and intimidating—encouraged Job? Reflect on a time you have felt encouraged by the Holy Spirit.

Connect

- Church teachers and leaders love to walk alongside Christ followers to answer tough questions about faith. Whether you are a visitor or a member of a local congregation, take them up on their open doors to assist you.

2. Recognize the enemy

I am sending you out like sheep among wolves. Therefore be as shrewd as snakes and as innocent as doves.

—MATTHEW 10:16

> We have a powerful enemy of the soul.
> But Satan is not God. He only knows and does
> what God permits in order to achieve God's purpose
> for us and God's final victory over evil.

If you want to know what matters to God, look where his enemy expends energy trying to thwart him.

Perhaps nothing on earth is as threatening to Satan as a new spirit, fresh from the breath of God. Nothing spells promise for God's plan like a newborn child and the deep bonds created in a growing family. Jesus came into the world that way.

Have you ever noticed—or experienced—that Satan and his accomplices are not satisfied with merely crippling God's beautiful creations? They throw everything they've got at bringing about a soul's total humiliation and demise.

In *The Screwtape Letters*, C.S. Lewis gives a fictional glimpse into the plausible inner workings of the demonic world, as an elder demon writes instructions for his nephew on how to secure souls for hell. "The overthrow of free peoples and the multiplication of slave-states are for us a means (besides, of course, being fun); but the real end is the destruction of individuals," Screwtape expounds. "For only individuals can be saved or damned, can become sons of the Enemy or food for us."[8]

The danger is that, as the descendants of Adam and Eve, we all have a tendency to distrust God or want to rule over him. If you have dedicated your life to Christ, then Satan has no hold on you. But even as your soul undergoes a day by day process of becoming more like Jesus, you have remnants of the fruit of the Fall, as Paul writes:

> So I find this law at work: When I want to do good, evil is right there with me. For in my inner being, I delight in God's law; but I see another law at work in the members of my body, waging war against the law of my mind and making me a prisoner of the law of sin at work within my members. What a wretched man I am! Who will rescue me from this body of death? Thanks be to God— through Jesus Christ our Lord (Romans 7:21-23).

We only have to get out of bed each day to see the many ways Satan, the Deceiver, deceives humankind (Revelation 12:9). For starters, he would like for us not to believe in his existence, and the godless culture around us fully complies. After all, if we are the gods of our lives, then we are in control, not some spiritual boogey-man leading us down a dark path. As a result of this thinking, comedians have had very successful careers making others laugh at biblical teaching about Satan.

In the 1970s, Flip Wilson had a hilarious gag where his character did something wrong, and he exclaimed, wide-eyed and in shock himself, "The devil made me do it!" That line became a favorite saying at the time. In the 80s and 90s Dana Carvey performed funny skits dressed up as "the church lady." With pursed lips, she accused people of wrong-doing under the influence of… "*Satan*, perhaps?!"

We can laugh at these funny guys, but the truth really is far from humorous when we witness the subtle but highly effective impact of evil, even among believers. The harshest words of Jesus were aimed directly at the most respected religious people of his day. "Woe to you, teachers of the law and Pharisees, you hypocrites! You travel over land and sea to win a single convert and when he becomes one, you make him twice as much a son of hell as you are" (Matthew 23:15). Another time he told them, "You belong to your father, the devil, and you want to carry out your father's desires" (John 8:44).

We have a powerful enemy of the soul because he is an enemy of God. Satan covets the things of God, and so he comes to steal and destroy—especially the Holy Spirit's sanctuary in a believing heart (John 10:10). But Satan is not equal to God. Only God is omniscient (all-knowing), omnipresent (everywhere at once), and omnipotent (most powerful of all), as we know from Deuteronomy 4:39, Psalm 139, Jeremiah 10:6, and the entire Bible and human experience.

So how does Satan fight? Typically, he and his army of demons try to steer us away from God through deceptions and lies, just as the serpent did with Eve (Genesis 3). They also enlist malleable hearts to carry out evil plans, as with Saul and Judas (1 Samuel, Matthew 26:14-15, John 13:27).

But God is sovereign over all, and he permits the enemy only to go as far as it serves God's people and God's plan, as with Job and Joseph and ourselves. Jesus used the enemy throughout his ministry to strengthen his disciples' faith and love. "Simon, Simon, Satan has asked to sift you as wheat," Jesus said. "But I have prayed for you, Simon, that your faith may not fail. And when you have turned back, strengthen your brothers" (Luke 22:31-32). Because Peter did indeed desert Jesus and was later restored through a mighty act of love and forgiveness, we have a Church today that is built on the rock-solid foundation of unfailing love (John 21:15-17).

Jesus also demonstrated God's physical power over evil spirits throughout his ministry, and they greatly feared him (Mark 5:1-13). So our focus should always remain on God. We can trust his Word as our first line of defense, the way Jesus did in the desert (Luke 4:1-13). And we can take comfort, as Jesus did, in knowing that God directs his heavenly army to protect us (Psalm 34:7, Psalm 91:11, Matthew 18:10).

Your marriage is a lynchpin, an outpost of promise against the devil's schemes, and so it will be tested for all it is worth. *Question everything.* Under the pressures in this life, when your spouse snaps at you about money or says something hurtful—intentionally or not—just see it for what it is: a tired soul worked on by the temptations within and the dark forces without.

If you feel menaced in this new phase, please realize it is because you are being menaced (Ephesians 6:12). Allow such moments of awareness to steer you into prayer, your substantive link with God and his power. And remember, as Jesus said, to "take heart," because his victory has been achieved (Luke 10:17-20, John 16).

Your new creation, a baby and mom and dad—the promise of your family—is a major force for good in God's world. The enemy doesn't like that, but he is no match for the one who lives in you or for the prayers whispered in Jesus' name (1 John 4:4). God's Spirit is constantly at work to help us overcome. He influences, shapes, and molds the most important part of us from the inside, out (John 14:15-27). It is the miracle of life with him.

Build & Grow

Learn

- Review Romans 7:21-23. Name a way you have recently experienced this inner conflict of opposing wills? How much conscious thought do you give to the reality of spiritual warfare in your daily life?

Absorb

- In Ephesians 6:10-18, Paul encourages believers to "put on the full armor of God" to equip us against the schemes of our enemy. What pieces of spiritual armor do you need to acquire or utilize for more personal victory?

Praise

- Your Christian family is a major force for good in God's world.

The enemy doesn't like that, but he is no match for the One who lives in you. Do you see evidence that your homelife can be a battlefield and target for the enemy? Pray the truth of 1 John 4:4 for your family.

Connect

- In following Christ, we all need mirrors, someone outside ourselves to reflect back who we are and help us lead an earnest life. If you struggle with a particular sin, find an accountability group through your church to have honest confessions and conversations about it on an ongoing basis. Or start a prayer group that meets weekly or monthly to help one another see God's truths in each other's lives.

3. Tether to truth

I remember the days of long ago;
I meditate on all your works
and consider what your hands have done.
I spread out my hands to you;
I thirst for you like a parched land.
Answer me quickly, Lord;
my spirit fails.

—PSALM 143:5-7

> Having a truthful, informed understanding about God and eternity is crucial for marriages and new parents because your grasp on reality will guide the way you live and teach.

"Will we have wings when we get to Heaven?" an eight year old asked in children's worship one Sunday. The uncertain look on his face pleaded, *"Surely not."* Children do ask the most revealing questions. It's a good thing, because they can grow into adults who hold vestiges of misguided views. Can you honestly think about God without seeing a man in a white robe and gray beard?

Having a truthful, informed understanding about God is crucial for new marriages and parents. Our picture of reality will guide the way we live and teach, because if we're going to be playing harps and singing all day when we get to Heaven, then maybe the alternative isn't so bad. Questioning becomes an extremely helpful antidote to this kind of spiritual drift. It is a lifeline.

So, what *does* the Bible—not the latest bestseller—actually say about Heaven? The truth is, not much. "Jesus' attitude to the other world is a sustained contradiction because his life reveals a radiant knowledge and his teaching preserves a rigid silence," John Watson observes.[9]

The Bible tells us that God will give us eternal pleasures at his right hand (Psalm 16:11). In the parable of the rich man and Lazarus (Luke 16), we see that Heaven is a comforting place, which Jesus called paradise (Luke 23:43). Jesus also promises that he is preparing a place for us there, in his Father's house, which has many rooms, and he will come back to take us there (John 14). He tells us we know the way: "I am the way and the truth and the life. No one comes to the Father except through me" (John 14:6).

But why does Jesus stop there? Why wouldn't God reveal more about the future life to really get us geared up and in line? We can only guess.

"Most likely Jesus recognized that frequent references to the circumstances of the unseen world would have obscured one of the chief points of his teaching," Watson suggests. "He was ever insisting that the Kingdom of Heaven was no distant colony in the clouds, but an institution set up in this present world."[10] Jesus said that he came so we may have life to the fullest (John 10:10), and the sense is that he means here and now as well as in eternity.

The entire Bible points to a fulfilling, meaningful life starting from the moment of belief and lasting forever in the presence of a loving Father. For now, that life means taking an active part in God's ever-renewing creations of marriage and family—our personal first-fruits. If Heaven is anything like the experience of finding a soul mate and together bringing a new life into the world, then we can expect an unimaginable Heaven. That could be the very reason Jesus didn't tell us more about it: we can't begin to fathom it. Even the angels erupted in praise when Jesus was born and God's plan revealed, so amazing and unexpected it was (Luke 2:13-14).[11]

"Many folk like to know beforehand what is to be set on the table,"

Gandalf told Frodo in *The Return of the King*. "But those who have labored to prepare the feast like to keep their secret; for wonder makes the words of praise louder."[12]

For now, we must remain vigilant with questioning. We live in a world where bad is called good, bondage is called freedom, and love is called hate. We see no end in sight to the perversion of basic logic and reason, and the assault on any who disagree. Physical facts are subjected to temporary feelings. Reality is malleable. Absurdly, like the book *1984* that George Orwell wrote in 1948, we are living in a time where truth is nonexistent because the world does not believe in it nor want it. Now, a "truth" evolves when a statement is proclaimed and repeated enough until everyone accepts it to be true.

For sanity's sake, and for our sincerest love of God, we must have a tether, a constant connection to truth in our lives. We are to consider the source of all that streams into our mind. "Test everything," Paul writes, and truly we must (1 Thessalonians 5:21).

Be selective about mentors, but be sure to find them—books, pastors, other believers with experience. All should stick to the Bible and its teaching. Nothing is to be added to it because it is the final word (Revelation 22:18-19, Proverbs 30:5-6). We are all students of someone, so listen and discern. Are the leaders in your life humble servants like Jesus? Are you? Loving, remembering, seeking, and questioning are actions that will serve you well in tethering to truth.

In a world such as we have today, perhaps the biggest question facing humankind is, "When will Jesus return?" It is his ultimate remaining promise to be fulfilled. More than once Jesus said we will not know. He advised that we live each day in anticipation of it, laboring under the yoke of God's mercy (Matthew 24:42, 25:13, and Mark 13:32-37). He then left a final question lingering over humankind: "However, when the Son of Man returns, will he find faith on the earth?" (Luke 18:8).

We will leave this chapter with encouraging words from our mentor Paul:

May God himself, the God of peace, sanctify you through and through. May your whole spirit, soul, and body be kept blameless at the coming of our Lord Jesus Christ. The one who calls you is faithful, and he will do it (1 Thessalonians 5:23-25).

Build & Grow

Learn

- For sanity's sake, and for our sincerest love of God, we must have a tether, a constant connection to truth in our lives. What are some common things the Bible labels as destructive, but that our culture calls good? What are some things the Bible labels as good but our culture opposes?

Absorb

- We are to consider the source of every piece of information that daily streams into our minds. "We demolish arguments and every pretension that sets itself up against the knowledge of God, and we take captive every thought to make it obedient to Christ" (2 Corinthians 10:5). How has questioning for the truth or the lack of questioning, shaped your view of God and your choices as a Christian? What are the results?

Praise

- Some of your growing family's best memories are likely to come from holiday celebrations and traditions. Santa Claus, the Easter Bunny, and other cultural influences are now attached to Christian celebrations for remembering and honoring God. Decide with your spouse how you plan to foster a holy reverence for such occasions in your family.

Connect

- As the world grows more alienated from truth, it grows more hostile to Christianity. Consciously bring people into your family life who are anchored in the truth of the Bible. Know the beliefs of the people who care for your children and the views they impart to them. Have frequent discussions around the family table, first without your children and later including them, about your beliefs and, as instances arrive, where they collide with worldly ways. Meanwhile, continue to be a light in the darkness for your community.

Plan Ahead

Choose points about Question to carry with you:

1.

2.

3.

Record a QUESTION gift for your child:

With good intentions, many expecting parents will buy a journal so they can write about their child's first days. Some then actually do it! But if you are not the journaling type, plan instead to have a simple notepad handy. Record the golden moments or spiritual curiosities in your child's life. Describe your gratitude for the way you see God supporting you in that season. As your child grows, record the questions asked and your answers. Jot down any spiritual markers you think might be meaningful for you to share later. In the future, you will be surprised at how much you forgot and yet how fun those memories are to re-live.

QUESTION early childhood board book connections:
Jesus Helps Me and *Close as a Breath*

Persevere

In God's design, "there is a time for everything and a season for every activity under the heavens." As you persevere, you give him opportunities to work in your life in unmistakable ways, to get to the other side, and to lead a peaceful family life through Jesus.

supplies to children waiting on the other side. At last a smaller, inexperienced engine arrives on the scene and surveys the sadness. The little engine thinks about the disappointed children. It decides surely it can do it. Fueled by repeating, "I think I can, I think I can," the engine strained to haul its load to the other side. And it did!

Children and adults today still love this version of the story adapted by Watty Piper first published in 1930.[1] It speaks to the potential little hero in all of us, who want to believe that we are capable of anything we set our minds to do. But the truth about the little engine and about all of us is that the mind is capable of very little if it is not motivated by the heart.

You've heard or maybe said, "My heart just wasn't in it," to explain giving up or performing poorly. And it's true: We tend to have no problem with persevering when we are doing so with our heart "in it." That goes for academic, athletic, and professional pursuits as well as those of romance, marriage, parenting, and faith. So, what puts a heart in it?

The world says, "visualize" the outcome you desire and set your mind to it. See yourself crossing the finish line first, then transfer your mental picture into your reality. Or, fuel your ambitions by optimism, and the "power of positive thinking" will carry you through to the happy place you desire. Still others will say to do the right thing and you will be rewarded. "Good karma" will bring you reciprocal acts at the right time.

But Jesus said to let go of the outcome and set your heart on God's desires. "But seek first the kingdom of God and his righteousness, and all these things will be added to you" (Matthew 6:33, ESV). God made us to have unique desires and goals. He simply asks us to prioritize him above it all in order to fulfill them. It's not as hard as it sounds. God has a specific plan for your life, and usually the very desires of your heart are tied to the gifts he gave you for your ultimate benefit and for his glory. When we permit God, he fuels our hearts with his love to apply them to the tasks at hand. And so, we have come full circle, because we know this kind of love is stronger than death—it never fails.

When you marry and when you have a child, *your heart is in it,* brimming with love. For this reason, your marriage and a new child present a double-whammy: two ideal passages of life for developing perseverance like never before, with fresh trials awaiting each day. It can be painful. We lose control over our world, the one with us at the center of it. Now other lives are involved and at stake. The days are challenging, spouses and babies unreasonable, and our own basic needs sometimes go wanting from neglect. Parents of a newborn barely have time to brush their teeth! Life can feel like one hurdle or mundane chore after another.

In the thick of all these challenges, it's hard to appreciate that you are benefitting from God-ordained circumstances that train your faith's ability to persevere, to get to the other side, and remain standing. That's important. A common thread running throughout the Old Testament is, "wait for the Lord; be patient and wait." After he came, the imperative became, "Don't give up!" Stand firm. All the New Testament writers stress perseverance, and Jesus himself urges it. He knows the scope of the epic war of which we are a part, whether we choose to be or not. He knows the trials we have and their meaning for our souls. He said:

Because of the love of wickedness, the love of most will grow cold, but he who stands firm to the end will be saved (Matthew 24:12).

All men will hate you because of me, but he who stands firm to the end will be saved (Matthew 10:22, Mark 13:13).

Be always on the watch and pray that you may be able to escape all that is about to happen, and that you may be able to stand before the Son of Man (Luke 21:36).

Only hold on to what you have until I come (Revelation 2:25).

Although salvation is a gift of the Lord, he clearly teaches that we have our part to do in cooperation with him, in the garden of our soul, even if we are only hanging on by our fingernails, as we sometimes are. God will help you, but you are not a puppet he can move with invisible strings. Muscles atrophy when not used, and the same is true of your spiritual muscle called *perseverance*. It gives you stamina to press ahead regardless of your physical realities. Using it gives you fortitude and makes your faith stronger and deeper as you come to realize it is God's power in you at work. There are no shortcuts, "because you know that the testing of your faith produces perseverance. Let perseverance finish its work so that you may be mature and complete, not lacking anything" (James 1:3-4).

God promised his chosen people a land of milk and honey. But he tasked them with fighting for it against brutal populations, with him leading the way. They balked, and then that generation spent the next 40 years consigned to a desert, never to enjoy God's plan (Exodus 13-14). Like them, our natural inclination is to take the path of least resistance. Much of our time is geared toward managing time and getting through it. We don't appreciate the broader implications of our current circumstances and their importance in different seasons, much less the gift of each day.

In God's order, "there is a time for everything, and a season for every activity under the heavens" (Ecclesiastes 3:1). The natural world and the spiritual world he created operate under his providence of seasons, achingly beautiful phases of life that must be lived for all they are worth in the moment. This side of life is comparatively short, and bizarrely speeds up as we get older. Each season matters because it eventually passes and will be gone forever, and the results of it become an inseparable part of eternity.

Jesus said, "Therefore, do not worry about tomorrow, for tomorrow will worry about itself. Each day has enough trouble of its own" (Matthew 6:34). At first these words have a grim reality. But Jesus addresses a tendency that can be crippling and overwhelming in difficult circumstances—looking too far ahead and imagining everything that can go wrong. This is especially true of expecting and new parents. Not only does this stifle spontaneous joy, but it also makes any challenge seem all the more difficult. When you find yourself straining under perseverance, you can be sure your circumstances are divinely keeping you in the moment.

When we savor the precious and fleeting seasons of a new child's life, we can patiently endure the more difficult phases. Each day has value, regardless of how menial the work might seem, because minute by minute we are building a home of eternal value. Parenting isn't a detour in your day or a distraction on the way to your life's ambition, it is the main road to realizing your worth. Here are only a few ways using it will help you and your new family:

Persevering overcomes doubt. Life does not always go the way we plan. When the pregnancy test is negative, or we get laid off from a job we worked so hard for, or when a child is born with a physical difficulty, doubts about God can be overwhelming.

Even John the Baptist, the person Jesus identified as the prophet preparing the Messiah's way, experienced serious doubt about who the Messiah was. John had led an austere life and fruitfully preached repentance. He was not expecting to end up in prison. We can sympathize. And Jesus did, too, as we can see from his encouraging words for and about John recorded in Matthew 11 and Luke 7.

Unexpected turns and suffering induce great strain on Christians. In the face of setbacks, illness, and other misfortunes, some even turn their backs on God and walk away. John could have done the same, and he probably would have been consoled and affirmed in doing so by his followers.

> "Humanity does not pass through phases as a train passes through stations: being alive, it has the privilege of always moving yet never leaving anything behind. Whatever we have been, in some sort we still are."
>
> —C.S. Lewis, *The Allegory of Love*

Jesus said, don't: "Blessed is he who does not fall away on account of me" (Matthew 11:6).

John persevered. He took his doubts directly to the Source, who, in kind, boldly encouraged him. We can be sure that John persevered to the tortuous end. His disciples buried him and reported his death to his Messiah. Hearing the news, Jesus went to a solitary place.

As you persevere under God's care, you give him opportunities to work in your life in unmistakable ways you never before could have imagined. He comes to the solitary place with you as you pray and grieve, and he picks you up again for another day.

Persevering overcomes evil. When we hit a hurdle with something we believe God has called us to do, we often take it as a sign that we are on the right track. That's right, the *right* track.

We daily pray for God's guidance and wisdom, and stay the course until we are sure that he is directing us to do otherwise. Then, the encouragement God sends *at just the right time*—in the form of unexpected good news, or relevant insights from Scripture, or the incisive words of another believer—keeps us going. And we need God's help. The system of this world is at war with God, so any good work important to God will encounter resistance. We all know this from personal experience, or eventually will, and it is writ large in the pages of the Bible.

Reading about the life of Joseph, starting in Genesis 37, we are appalled by the relentless march of evil in his life—for decades. He was stripped and sold into slavery by his jealous brothers, who then told their father that Joseph was mauled to death by a wild animal. As a slave down in Egypt, Joseph was framed by a seductress and unjustly imprisoned by her husband. Then, he was forgotten by a fellow prisoner he helped free. Years went by.

Joseph's life was a saga of perseverance while trusting God, and it resulted in nothing less than the survival of the 12 tribes of Israel and the expansion of God's kingdom on earth to this day. "You intended to harm me, but God intended it for good to accomplish what is now being done, the saving of many lives," Joseph told his brothers (Genesis 50:20). How true. When you persevere with God in the face of evil, you are doing exactly the same thing. The victorious ripple affect will be felt for generations after you.

Persevering overcomes despair. One of the results of persevering through difficult times with God at your side, is the unmistakable recognition of his love in your life. Comforting personal experiences that can only be explained by his presence, lead to deeper gratitude and love for him, which helps overcome the despair caused by the circumstance. Though we prefer it had never happened, we grow to appreciate the outcome God gives us as a result of it.

Our pastor has a 15-year-old son who has never spoken a word and has severe functional limits. The child was healthy and well until he turned two, when he experienced cerebral episodes that are undiagnosed to this day, even after examinations by doctors all over the country. The pastor, his wife, and their daughter have endured great hardship as a result. They have questioned God and been deeply discouraged as they watched their dreams for their family die one by one.

But just a few Sundays ago, he said he wouldn't trade his life—nor his son—for anything. He dearly loves his son and has seen God's love in his life in profound ways. At minimum, our pastor's hardship has made him a tremendous pastor leading a thriving, impactful church. An outpouring of support for the pastor's family resulted in a special needs ministry that was one of the first of its kind in the nation. Many more exist today as a result, serving a highly neglected segment within the Church.

"I am sorry for the Christian who has not something in his circumstances he wishes was not there," Oswald Chambers writes.[2] Going through trials under God's care brings a heavenly presence to this side of life that we would not otherwise know. You can't viscerally know what that is like until you actually experience it.

Despair happens when we feel like we don't have any options or that our suffering is pointless or punishment. In Christ, we take heart. No tears will go to waste, no injustices will go unanswered, no defeats will result in death. "No, in all these things we are more than conquerors through him who loved us" (Romans 8:37).

Applying It in Marriage and Family Life

Are you ready? There's no time like the present to exercise your ability to persevere under God's loving care:

- **Stay safe in the fold.** Sheep find safety in numbers, and you can, too, by avoiding the spiritual hazard of isolation.

- **Lean on the faithful.** Draw encouragement from the true accounts of everyday people who have prevailed in trials and suffering.

- **Keep it simple.** Pace yourself and accept Jesus' invitation to a more satisfying, restful life with him.

Before moving on, keep in mind that a highly effective resource God gave you for persevering is laughter. It is one of the most natural human reflexes. In addition to its well-documented health benefits, laughing generates a second wind for perseverance.[3] Be sure to keep a good sense of humor in your arsenal. It often helps when all else fails.

1. Stay safe in the fold

Very truly I tell you, I am the gate for the sheep. All who have come before me are thieves and robbers, but the sheep have not listened to them. I am the gate; whoever enters through me will be saved. They will come in and go out, and find pasture. The thief comes only to steal and kill and destroy; I have come that they may have life, and have it to the full. I am the good shepherd.

—JOHN 10:7-11

Joining a church that pleases God and resonates with both your spouse and your soul is vital. It is there, not in the world, where your family will find reinforcement to persevere.

People today tend to view the word *religion* in a negative light. It evokes images of imposing duties, meaningless rituals, and insincere obligations. From history we can observe how the Jews' religious practices—so vital for their institutional memory, spiritual defense, and training as God's people—were twisted by religious leaders, the wolves of Jesus' day, to keep their lock on power and privilege. Their experience is only too familiar, having been repeated throughout Christian history, as well. Today many will say, "I'm not religious, but I believe in God."

In its purest meaning as a system of belief and worship, however, religion is exactly what we need to persevere in marriage and parenting. Having fellowship and worshipping with other believers is God's idea. But it means much more than a building. It is a Presence. Jesus said, "...And on this rock I will build my church, and the gates of Hades will not overcome it" (Matthew 16:18).

Paul teaches, "His intent was that now, through the church, the manifold wisdom of God should be made known to the rulers and authorities in the heavenly realms, according to his eternal purpose that he accomplished in Christ Jesus our Lord" (Ephesians 3:10-11). In our time, Christians commonly use lower c "church" to refer to the local place we go. We use "the Church" to refer to the movement of God's plan advanced by the Body of Christ.

Being part of a church that pleases God and resonates with both your spouse and your soul is a vital aim. It is there, not in the world, where your family will find reinforcement to persevere. Through sermons, your pastor will unfold teachings from the Bible that are like new pieces of equipment that prepare and protect you. Relationally, you can connect with others at the same stage in life, and start a small group so you can grow and support each other through life changes. Your growing faith community will bring a trustworthy circle of teachers, role models, and friends into your child's spiritual life. Sheep find safety in their flock. Getting separated makes them afraid. Safety in numbers holds true for people—especially parents—in the spiritual world, too.

As we discussed in *Remember,* part of your job entering marriage is to sort out your experiences and preferences regarding faith. In practice, some people prefer liturgy and structure. Some don't. Some prefer traditional music and others prefer contemporary. But one thing is for sure, worshiping together is a spiritually beneficial practice. "Let the message of Christ dwell among you richly as you teach and admonish one another with all wisdom through psalms, hymns, and songs from the Spirit, singing to God with gratitude in your hearts" (Colossians 3:16).

There are no right answers or perfect churches because there are no perfect people. So it's best to be humble and earnest about what you likewise bring to the table and can contribute (Romans 12:3-8). One approach is to major on the majors (e.g. Jesus is God incarnate) and minor on the minors. That is, be sure the message is true to the Bible, but be flexible about secondary issues like music style or whether or not pastors wear robes.

Maybe the reason Jesus permits the many branches, denominations, and sects of his Church is to prevent the greater evil that would occur if one institution held a monopoly over humankind's knowledge of him. An institution can become a tyrant. We know from history that with any enterprise, "power tends to corrupt and absolute power corrupts absolutely."[4] Maybe the church variety is just a natural outcome of God's creative work. One of the beautiful aspects of humanity is the breath-taking variety within it.

Whatever the reason, we have a great variety of Christian fellowship and worship styles today. Human destiny marches on, and we know without a doubt what our eyes see: the Church, with Christ at the head, is a heavenly force achieving God's plan by persevering to make disciples of all the nations. The Church works with amazing versatility, purpose, and creativity, and just like the parts of the human body, every aspect plays its part for the glory of God and the benefit of its members (1 Corinthians 12).

> "For Jesus Christ alone is our unity. 'He is our peace.' Through him alone do we have access to one another, joy in one another, and fellowship with one another."
>
> —Dietrich Bonhoeffer, *Life Together*

Just remember that your "religion" is an external feature. It can offer, organize, encourage, and help fulfill the Christian life, but it is not in itself the Christian life. Outward activities do not take the place of a personal inner relationship with God, which is vital for shaping your priorities and influencing your daily life. Being clear on this distinction with your children as they grow will convey where the heart of faith lies—in a person, not a building or rituals. That way, they have the freedom to reject your worship traditions without also rejecting God or you.

Spiritual journeys are by nature "seeking in progress," and they are persistently personal. You, your spouse, and child might rarely be at the same place, spiritually, at the same time. Meanwhile, your bonds will be tested by outside forces, like work demands, and inner forces, like selfish desires. Don't go through life alone. God will help you persevere through all your days like nothing else can, within the safety of his Body. Your family's and the Church's ability to stand will confirm his work.

Build & Grow

Learn

- Read Paul's description of the church as a Body in 1 Corinthians 12. What is the main point in each paragraph? This discussion of the church is the lead-in to his famous description of love in chapter 13. How do these two discussions relate to one another?

Absorb

- How does thinking of your family as Christ's body affect the way you and your spouse view one another's strengths and weaknesses? How will having a child affect your "family body"?

Praise

- Because there are no perfect people, there are no perfect churches. The parking situation, the sermon, the song quality, the volume, the crying babies, the style of clothes people wear, the slow check-in at the nursery, the manners—you get the idea. Church workers can grow very discouraged with the complaints. Stop yourself when you feel a criticism coming on. Instead, be part of the solution through helpful, loving acts. Reach out! Tell a pastor or volunteer how much you appreciate their work. Praise God that you have a church!

Connect

- A big frustration for new parents is that they are too busy with a new baby to be involved with their church as before, worship as a couple, or stay connected to friends. Before your child arrives, reach out to others in your church in a similar life stage. Meet regularly so you can walk together, share real struggles through prayer requests, and receive godly support. And remember, this is a season, a temporary stage. You'll experience some uniquely precious moments and some tough phases. Both will pass with time and give way to a new season. Remember the stages do not last forever, so hold onto the good, even as you endure the parts that are hard for you.

2. Lean on the faithful

Therefore, since we are surrounded by such a great cloud of witnesses, let us throw off everything that hinders and the sin that so easily entangles. And let us run with perseverance the race marked out for us, fixing our eyes on Jesus, the pioneer and perfecter of faith. For the joy set before him he endured the Cross, scorning its shame, and sat down at the right hand of the throne of God. Consider him who endured such opposition from sinners, so that you will not grow weary and lose heart.

—Hebrews 12:1-3

Perseverance demonstrates love for God and others like nothing else can. Draw encouragement to persevere by studying the spiritual chronicles of others and claim them as your brothers and sisters in Christ.

While our physical lives have great variety from person to person, they have common organs and systems that make them human bodies. The same is true of our spiritual lives. We are individually unique, yet all spirits have common functionalities that make them spirits. That's why we can draw much encouragement to persevere by studying the spiritual journeys of others and claiming them as our brothers and sisters. We find something intimately familiar about them.

We often use the terms *characters* and *Bible stories*, as if biblical accounts are fictional. But they involve everyday flesh and blood people with real challenges. No human imagination could make that stuff up! We see their struggles and their losses. But we also see their eventual fruits from working cooperatively with God.

Jesus said, "But the seed on good soil stands for those with a noble and good heart, who hear the word, retain it, and by persevering produce a crop" (Luke 8:15). You probably know people like this in your own life. How do they have this good soil that produces a noble and good heart? We can glean insights from a few familiar historical figures.

When we first meet Job, David, and Mary in the pages of Bible history, we can understandably be impressed. They are already heroic. Job possesses a mighty faith, one that God trusts will prevent Job from rejecting him when Job's fortunes changed. And He didn't!

With David, we see a lanky teen who steps up to face the giant who has everyone else trembling. His weak appearance insulted his foe Goliath. Yet David demanded: *Who is this uncircumcised Philistine that he should defy the armies of the living God?* Then he took Goliath out!

Mary hears the news from Gabriel that she is highly favored by God and will have God's child, the Messiah. Though shocked, she said, "I am the Lord's servant. May it be to me as you have said." Mary delivered the Savior of the world!

We can similarly admire the boldness of well-known Christians throughout time. But what is hidden from our view is all that took place before they walked into the pages of history—the years of perseverance that tilled the soil for their noble and good hearts. We don't see their daily steps involving obedience, gumption, and failures.

Unlike a straight line from A to Z, Christian spiritual development is often like an ever-upward spiral. The path circles back, sometimes painfully, to cover old ground, so we can review and practice what we've learned. But the path also goes onward and upward with diligence. If you think your soil is good now, just wait! God has more in store for you. And you will be forever grateful, because it enables you to humbly chart the heights to which he wants to bless you and your new family.

An unseasoned character could not have endured the devastation we witness Job endure. Before encountering Goliath, David's life was one marked by steady reliability in life's chores and routines, which armed him with a life-saving trust in God. We read that as a teen, Mary had already found favor with God when visited by his chief representative. As a teen! How did she do that? Surely, humble obedience and perseverance. Her noble and good heart was costly. But today, we do indeed still call her blessed (Luke 1:48).

When you consider that your life, your marriage, and your child are as important to God as Job's and David's and Mary's, you understand that you have the same standing with God. You have the same power to persevere—and prevail—as they and so many others have. You see how God works in many different ways to achieve his good purpose, and you remember that you are not alone. He is with you:

> And we boast in the hope of the glory of God. Not only so, but we also glory in our sufferings, because we know that suffering produces perseverance; perseverance, character; and character, hope. And hope does not put us to shame, because God's love has been poured out into our hearts through the Holy Spirit, who has been given to us (Romans 5:2-4).

Search out narratives about the lives of others who have persevered for the faith. Read and re-read the ones that strike a chord with you and dwell with them. These beacons from throughout time will become your mentors, good company calling you onward and upward. Their glimmering testimonies of perseverance could fill an evening sky. Yours will become one of them, and the only one exactly like it.

Build & Grow

Learn

- Bring to mind one challenge or trial you are facing now and then look to examples in the Bible for perseverance. For example:
  - Are you struggling with health? Write out Paul's response to the "thorn in his flesh" (2 Corinthians 2:10).

- Are you facing an insurmountable battle with a figurative giant? Write out David's response to Goliath the day of the battle (1 Samuel 17:45-47).

- Do you have doubt and confusion in the midst of your God-ordained circumstances? Write out Mary's song after conceiving Christ through the Holy Spirit (Luke 1:46-55).

- Something else? Search the concordance in the back of your Bible and discover new references for any challenge.

Absorb

• Do you tend to see Bible figures as real people with real emotions, or as just fictional examples? Which ones stand out to you? Think about the struggles they faced and how those very hardships later led to their victorious faith. How are your hardships strengthening your personal ties with God?

Praise

• Take time to consider specific trials you have had, and reflect on the character-shaping benefits that you reaped. In what ways did God encourage you?

Connect

• We can draw much encouragement to persevere by studying the spiritual journeys of others and claiming them as our brothers and sisters. Search out narratives about the lives of those who have persevered for the faith with joy and thanksgiving. Make familiarity with them a part of your family's culture. These beacons from throughout time will become old family friends, good company calling you all onward and upward.

3. Keep it simple

Come to me, all you who are weary and burdened, and I will give you rest. Take my yoke upon you and learn from me, for I am gentle and humble in heart, and you will find rest for your souls. For my yoke is easy, and my burden is light.

—MATTHEW 11:28-30

> Jesus introduced an entirely new perspective by teaching beyond the letter of the law to the spirit of it. His often-repeated lesson was that the inner state of a person matters more than anything else.

People once thought the best way to teach a child to swim was to toss him into the water and watch him flail around until he figured it out. Being in a new marriage or becoming a first-time parent can feel *just like that*—diving into unknown waters and then bobbing up and down at times, gasping for air. Older relatives give you a "welcome to the world" grin. Sometimes they offer to help.

Having a child is a life-altering event, starting as soon as you get that positive test result or adoption approval.

Whether this one moment in time releases joyful emotion or unwelcomed shock, it will open the door to a whole new level of activity, planning, questioning, and yes, sometimes even flailing. It's easy to feel that way when you enter a brand new season of life. Then, nothing beats having a reliable friend to help you with the physical and emotional needs. And nothing beats your Savior in meeting your spiritual ones.

When Jesus came to earth, family life existed under the oppressive yoke of religious and political duties. In striking contrast to the convoluted regulations of his day, Jesus presented a picture of life with God that was sublimely simple. His godly talent was to transform the artificially complex into practical, if blunt, truths that were like nothing the people had ever heard before.[5]

With his Beatitudes and the Sermon on the Mount, Jesus upended centuries of complex rule-making, ceremonial fetishes, and fiats that lavished duties on the outside of the cup, but left the inside insidiously tainted (Matthew 5-7).

> "May our Lord Jesus Christ himself and God our Father, who loved us and by his grace gave us eternal encouragement and good hope, encourage your hearts and strengthen you in every good deed and word....May the Lord direct your hearts into God's love and Christ's perseverance."
>
> —2 Thessalonians 2:16-17, 3:5

After Jesus finished his Sermon, Matthew observed, "the crowds were amazed at his teaching, because he taught as one who had authority, and not as their teachers of the law" (7:28-29).

Jesus impressed his listeners by going beyond the letter of the law to the spirit of it. His repeated lesson was that the inner life of a person mattered more to God than the external life. "You have heard that it was said, 'You shall not commit adultery,'" Jesus said. "But I tell you that anyone who looks at a woman lustfully has already committed adultery with her in his heart." (Matthew 5:27-28).

Today, we slavishly tend to external circumstances at the expense of our inner life. The rulers, powers, and authorities of this world prefer it that way (Ephesians 6:10). If we busy ourselves with the externals, making sure they satisfy us, we don't have much time or need for the internals. But the inner space shrivels with its meager diet. Its defenses weaken, and a heart becomes vulnerable to temptation and illness. When disaster strikes, that spirit is crushed.

Jesus brought to ailing, distracted humanity the perfect remedy. "Martha, Martha, you are worried and upset about many things," he said, "but few things are needed—or indeed only one. Mary has chosen what is better, and it will not be taken away from her" (Luke 10:38-42). Martha had complained about her unhelpful sister who was listening at the feet of Jesus. Martha was still learning his new ways. Casting off the old yoke and taking on the new one requires time.

We all permit ourselves to get similarly sidetracked. The seasons of life-change, and even those of abundance, can easily distract or consume all of our energy. Life pulls us in many directions with the demands of new children, work pressures, and so many ways to fritter away our time. We make things more complicated than they need to be.

But a life intentionally ordered around matters of the spirit brings reality into focus from the core. Don't you love the sweet simplicity and assurance Jesus offers for filling it?

Capping his Sermon on the Mount, he said, "Therefore everyone who hears these words of mine and puts them into practice is like a wise man who built his house on the rock. The rain came down, the streams rose, and the winds blew and beat against that house; yet it did not fall, because it had its foundation on the rock" (Matthew 7:24-25).

Even though you cannot see, touch, or hear Jesus in the physical way now, you can choose to take on his yoke and rest at his feet. You can love the things Jesus loves. Remember the things he remembers. Seek the things he seeks. Question the things he questions. And persevere for all that he perseveres. Day by day you will become more like him. As you do, your marriage will experience God's power and peace, and your child will be blessed.

Build & Grow

Learn

- The external life can keep you busy, distracted, and burdened by your problems. Read Matthew 11:28-30. Name a few burdens, and wearisome situations you are ready to turn over to God. Why does God invite us by saying, "my yoke is easy, and my burden is light"?

Absorb

- Today we slavishly tend to external circumstances at the expense of our inner life. Maybe we hit the gym regularly, throw ourselves into a hobby, and effectively tend to our career growth. If the inner life matters more to God than the outer life, does your focus match his? How is your inner condition outwardly evident?

Praise

- In striking contrast to the convoluted regulations of his day, Jesus presented a picture of life with God that was sublimely simple. His godly talent was to transform the artificially complex into practical, if hard, truths. Before baby arrives, ask God to show you where you can simplify, make space, and find more rest to be with him.

Connect

- Given the full-time demands a new child brings, make the commitment now to set aside a weekly date night with your spouse once the baby is settled into a routine. Work out reliable, trustworthy childcare needed to make that happen. Sticking to the commitment will be a strong sign of love. At first you might have a hard time not talking about the baby! Be patient with each other. Reconnect with the reasons you are together. Continue to dream about the possibilities ahead.

Plan Ahead

Choose points about PERSEVERE that are important to you:

1.

2.

3.

Curate a PERSEVERE gift for your child:

Music is a gift that refreshes and soothes the soul. Before your baby arrives, make a collection of your favorite spiritual songs to share as early as the delivery room. Choose lyrics that build faith and speak truth about God. Make such songs a routine part of the day, like during feedings, before naptime, or in the car together. Music is a great way to help your child worship and connect with God from the earliest days and is sure to help you persevere, too.

PERSEVERE early childhood board book connections:
Jesus Invites Me and *Little Seed: A Life*

Now What?

When we first came home with our new little bundle, our first thought was, "Now what do we do?" Fewer moments in life have more emphatically announced, "You have no idea what you are doing!" It was a humbling awareness of a huge new responsibility.

We've found that even now, no matter how well our children grow, we encounter frequent trials of trust, both in our abilities as parents and in God. Now that you have worked through *your* newborn promise project, we want to encourage you once more that you are not alone, and leave you with a few next steps for using what you've planned.

Connect with Other Parents

Being a new parent is a great equalizer. This new stage in life overcomes boundaries, like professional status, that before would have been barriers to friendship with others in your neighborhood or even your church. Nothing builds kinship like discussing diapers and breastfeeding! We've offered many suggestions for connecting with other parents. If you haven't already, please take that step.

One mom we know started "Blanket Babies," inviting people in our community with newborns to meet weekly at a local park. We were grateful for her initiative. The moms exchanged stories and information while the newborns observed. Eventually, those babies were sitting up and then toddling. A group like this can be a lifeline to bring you out of isolation into a genuine community. Also, joining or starting a small group at your church is vital. You can share the highs and lows with biblical support, growing your faith and parenting abilities along the way. Organizing it around *Your Newborn Promise Project Group Study* is a natural next step that will enrich your parenting life in community (see last pages).

Start Your Child's Newborn Promise Project

What's true for grownups about the spiritual life is true for children, too, because life with God is remarkably coherent. His Word is a gift to the soul, and so reading it is a primary gateway for growing more like him—and a primary gateway for your child's spiritual formation from the very beginning.

We recommend reviewing the early childhood Newborn Promise resources at the end of this book, and start with your child from birth. Your infant will benefit from the sound of your voice, and you will benefit from being grounded in the spiritual basics. In the process, you audibly stake a claim against the powers of this world that your child belongs to Jesus. You train yourself to think about Jesus like your child will, a transformation that is vital to your own relationship with him (Matthew 18:2-4). As your child grows, you will learn, absorb, and praise together, asking and answering faith's—life's—biggest questions along the way.

Remember to Reflect

Over time, your family's experiences will continue to shape your spiritual lives. We hope that your soul-searching work on your Newborn Promise Project will be fruitful for the days and years to come.

But some days we don't feel so new or promising. If you ever feel spiritually dry or adrift, revisit these pages and your reflections on them. The hopes and plans you have recorded will be an anchor, bringing you back home to the things that matter most. It is a good place for the mind to be. You will also see how far you've come! From that vantage point, you'll find much encouragement and gratitude.

Before you go, let us shower you with a parent dedication, a send-off that is God's promise for us all:

As the rain and the snow
  come down from heaven,
and do not return to it
  without watering the earth
and making it bud and flourish,
  so that it yields seed for the sower and bread for the eater,
so is my word that goes out from my mouth:
  It will not return to me empty,
but will accomplish what I desire
  and achieve the purpose for which I sent it.
You will go out in joy
  and be led forth in peace;
the mountains and hills
  will burst into song before you,
and all the trees of the field
  will clap their hands.
Instead of the thornbush will grow the juniper,
  and instead of briers the myrtle will grow.
This will be for the LORD's renown,
  for an everlasting sign,
  that will endure forever.

—Isaiah 55:10-13

Notes

Love

1. Saint Thérèse of Lisieux, *The Story of a Soul* (New York: Doubleday, 2001), p. 63.

2. Ibid., p. 63.

3. Mark Roskill, editor, *The Letters of Vincent Van Gogh* (New York: Atheneum, 1963), p. 287.

4. Benjamin Franklin, *Poor Richard's Almanack,* December 1751.

5. Dallas Willard, *Renovation of the Heart: Putting on the Character of Christ* (Colorado Springs, CO: NavPress, 2002), p. 29.

6. Marvin R. Wilson, *Our Father Abraham: Jewish Roots of the Christian Faith* (Grand Rapids, Michigan: William B. Eerdmans Publishing Company, 1989), p. 202.

7. Ibid, p. 202.

8. John Watson, *The Mind of the Master* (New York: Dodd, Mead and Company, 1897), p. 170-171.

9. C. S. Lewis, *The Four Loves* (New York: Harcourt, Brace, 1960), The Family Christian Library special edition, p. 277.

10. General Douglas MacArthur, from his speech "Duty, Honor, Country," delivered at his acceptance of the Sylvanus Thayer Award on May 12, 1962 at West Point. Available at http://www.american-rhetoric.com.

11. Fulton J. Sheen quote from Benedict J. Groeschel, *The Journey Toward God: In the Footsteps of the Great Spiritual Writers* (Ann Arbor, MI: Charis Books, 2000), p. 80.

Remember

1. Numerous studies confirm the great capacity of prenatal and

newborn children to absorb from their surroundings. For two respected findings, refer to:

> Anne Fernald, Virginia A. Marchman, and Adriana
> Weisleder, "SES in language processing skill and vocabu-
> lary are evident at 18 months," *Developmental Science*, 16:2
> (2013), p. 234-248.
>
> Christine Moon, Hugo Lagercrantz, and Patricia K. Kuhl,
> "Language experienced in utero affects vowel perception
> after birth: a two-country study," Acta Paediatrica, 102:2
> (February 2013), p. 156-160.

2. Policy Statement from the American Academy of Pediatrics,
June 2014, "Literacy Promotion: An Essential Component of
Primary Care Pediatric Practice," Council on Early Childhood; pub-
lished in *Pediatrics*, 134:2, August 2014.

3. Thomas F. Torrance, *The Christian Doctrine of God* (Scotland:
T&T Clark Ltd., 1996), p. 89.

4. A. W. Tozer, *Knowledge of the Holy* (New York: Harper Collins,
1978), p. 17.

5. Ibid, p. 17.

6. Marvin R. Wilson, *Our Father Abraham: Jewish Roots of the
Christian Faith* (Grand Rapids: William B. Eerdmans Publishing Co.,
1989), p. 161.

7. "Evangelism Is Most Effective Among Kids," The Barna Group,
a study released October 11, 2004.

8. Yosef Hayim Yerushalmi, *Zakhor: Jewish History and Jewish
Memory* (Washington: University of Washington Press, 1996), p. 9.

Seek

1. C. S. Lewis, *The Problem of Pain* (New York: Touchstone, 1996),
p. 132.

2. Alfred Edersheim, *The Life and Times of Jesus the Messiah*

(Hendrickson Publishers, 1993), Book Three, page 402.

3. *The Problem of Pain*, p. 132.

4. Saint Teresa of Avila, *Interior Castle: The Soul's Spiritual Journey to Union with God* (Alachua, FL: Bridge-Logos, 2008), p. 22.

5. Ibid, p. 21.

6. Brother Lawrence, *The Practice of the Presence of God: The Best Rule of a Holy Life* (New York: Fleming H. Revell Company, 1895), p. 9.

7. Ibid, p. 20.

8. Frank C. Laubach, *Letters by a Modern Mystic* (Colorado Springs, CO: Purposeful Design Publications, 2007), p. 75.

9. Ibid, p. 78, 56.

10. Dallas Willard, *Renovation of the Heart: Putting on the Character of Christ* (Colorado Springs, CO: NavPress, 2002), p. 152.

11. Josh McDowell, *The New Evidence That Demands a Verdict* (Nashville, TN: Thomas Nelson Publishers, 1999), chapters 3, 4, and 21.

Question

1. From Aleksandr Solzhenitsyn's play, *Candle in the Wind*, 1960; translated by Keith Armes, 1973.

2. From Mark Twain's nonfiction, *Following the Equator: A Journey Around the World*, 1897, chapter 15 epigraph quoting "Pudd'nhead Wilson's New Calendar."

3. Thomas F. Torrance, *The Christian Doctrine of God* (Scotland: T&T Clark Ltd., 1996), p. 19.

4. Ibid.

5. John Watson, *The Mind of the Master* (New York: Dodd, Mead and Company, 1897), p. 56.

6. A. W. Tozer, *Knowledge of the Holy* (New York: Harper Collins,

1978), p. viii.

7. Ray C. Stedman, *Let God Be God: Life Changing Truths from the Book of Job* (Grand Rapids, MI: Discovery House Publishers, 2007), p. 46.

8. C. S. Lewis, *The Screwtape Letters* (New York: HarperOne, 1996), p. 207.

9. John Watson, *The Mind of the Master* (New York: Dodd, Mead and Company, 1897), p. 297.

10. Ibid., p. 299.

11. *The Christian Doctrine of God,* p. 19.

12. J. R. R. Tolkein, *Return of the King* (Boston: Mariner Books, 1994), p. 949.

Persevere

1. Watty Piper, *The Little Engine That Could* (New York: Platt & Munk, 1930).

2. Oswald Chambers, *My Utmost for His Highest* (Uhrichsville, OH: Barbour Publishing, Inc., special edition), May 19.

3. Numerous scientific studies have charted the physical health benefits of laughing. But perhaps first-hand experience is the best gauge of all, and positive proof of laughter's mental health benefits, too.

4. Lord Acton (John Emerich Edward Dalbert-Acton), from his letter to Bishop Mandell Creighton, April 5, 1887; collected in *Essays on Freedom and Power,* edited by Gertrude Himmelfarb, 1949, public domain.

5. Alfred Edersheim, *The Life and Times of Jesus the Messiah* (Hendrickson Publishers, 1993), gives a detailed and vivid account of Jewish laws and customs, and the collision they met with Jesus.

From the Authors

Not long after introducing the first of its kind Learn, Absorb & Praise™ Christian board book collection for children ages 0 to 7, we recognized a gap in support for their moms and dads, too, as they step into entirely new roles as parents and enter a new phase in marriage and their individual development.

We devoted the next year to talking with parents, pastors, and teachers about how to best guide expecting and new parents in this major life transition—both its challenges and its divinely appointed potential. We prayed a lot.

For two more years, we continued as students. We studied what the Bible had to say about our relationship with God and with each other. There, we immersed in the experiences of others and listened to God's instruction. We reflected on our own marriages and parenting experiences, and God's work through them.

Often during the course of this work, we were in the midst of the very challenges we were writing about. We juggled schedules, went through parenting crises with our children, and worked among laundry baskets and other routines of daily life. As of this writing, our extended team has brought five new lives into the world, experienced miscarriage, infertility, problem pregnancy, sent kids to college, moved to new cities, and experienced unsolvable medical issues and the death of parents. Our family lives are just like yours.

Along the way, the Newborn Promise Project kept us focused on our loving God. We have all been changed by the process, and we pray that you will be changed by it, too. We will always be students with you, on this great adventure of everlasting life together.

—*Callie Grant, Audra Haney, Charissa Kolar, August 2017*

Working for publishers like Scholastic and Dorling Kindersley, Callie developed creative educational content to build children's literacy and learning skills. It wasn't until she had a child of her own that she appreciated how important reading from birth is—for cognitive, emotional, and spiritual development. In 2011, she launched Graham Blanchard to create Christian board books and parenting resources for new families growing up in God. Callie lives in Austin, Texas, with her husband, Michael, and their daughter.

Audra has written and produced quality Christian broadcast content for a wide range of audiences across the globe. But after welcoming her first child in 2014 and navigating the new (and sometimes choppy) waters of parenting, Audra decided to combine her media-life and mom-life to reach out to her favorite audience yet: expecting and new parents. Audra co-produces and hosts the Newborn Promise Podcast. She lives in Knoxville, Tennessee, with her husband, Cory, a missions pastor, and their two daughters.

Charissa joined the original start-up team at Graham Blanchard as an editorial advisor for child and parent content. Today, she continues program development and co-produces the Newborn Promise Podcast. Charissa also combines her passion for the spiritual development of families with her extensive communications background to write about the adventures—and often humorous mishaps—of parenting two energetic boys alongside her husband, Rob. Her family lives in the San Francisco East Bay Area.

The Newborn Promise Project Collection

Small Groups and Classes

As Christian faith thrives in community, the Group Study offers an enriching dimension to the personal assessment and planning of husband and wife. Whether in a church class or small group, this study illuminates the common bonds of growing families and brings them together on the sublimely simple path with Jesus.

Your Newborn Promise Project Group Study
Paperback, $8.99, 6 x 9 inches, 96 pages
ISBN 9780989794992

Newborn Promise Podcast

Join author Audra Haney and friends each week to navigate your growing family's spiritual life with the support of other parents well-regarded in their fields. Series cover topics from Building Your Family to After the Baby Arrives, with first-hand accounts that will guide and inspire the spiritual vitality of families in transition. Available at grahamblanchard.com, through the Newborn Promise Project App, and on Google Play and iTunes.

Coloring and Activity Book

Young children can start thinking about their own Newborn Promise and what life in the Spirit means for them. Led by the Knowing My God series Soul Mates, your child will color, imagine, draw, write, solve, and dream their way through creative applications of the grown-up Primer. For ages 4 & up.

Your Newborn Promise Project Wings
Paperback, $6.99, 8.5 x 11 inches, 32 pages
ISBN 9780692850336

The Newborn Promise Project Collection

"The power of these resources lies in their ability to help forge much-needed community among moms and dads. That is the most significant thing that can happen for parents as they seek to grow in their faith."

—Brian Wallace, Executive Director, Fuller Formation Groups, Fuller Theological Seminary

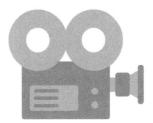

Your Newborn Promise True Story Videos

FREE! With Primer or Group Study book purchase. Use coupon code NPPCHW at www.grahamblanchard.com to download artfully produced videos featuring couples who share their experiences as new parents building faith.

Newborn Promise App

Expecting and new parents have automatic access to ideas, inspiration, and podcast updates through a beautiful interface available on all devices.

What is Your Faith Style?

Take the quiz at grahamblanchard.com and find out why it matters.

Early Childhood Books With Newborn Promise

The first years of a child's life are the most important time for cognitive, social, and emotional development, and are essential for establishing a lifelong love for Jesus. The spiritual abilities explored in the Newborn Promise parenting resources—**Love**, **Remember**, **Seek**, **Question**, **Persevere**— naturally correlate with the basic Biblical concepts in our board books. Reading them together from the start strengthens family ties as infant, mom, and dad build and grow together in their faith.

Love

Created in God's Image

Because we are created in God's image, love creates a spiritual bond, not a physical one. Family bonds are primarily spiritual unions of love. The Bible describes love best. Look closely at what God says about love: *Jesus Shows Me*, the Knowing My God series (ISBN 9780985409036) and *Your Core* (ISBN 9780985409050).

Remember

A Friend to Faith

When we are rooted and established in Jesus, time is a friend to faith. As we grow, we carry memories of how God has revealed himself in our personal lives and in the human history of the Bible. The family of God creates loving memories with him: *All of Me That You Can't See* (ISBN 9780985409043) and *To The Sea* (ISBN 9780989794947).

Early Childhood Books With Newborn Promise

Seek

The Protecting Thirst

A soul must be nurtured by its Source. Seeking is the steady effort we make to grow in closeness with God. We discover along the way that our spiritual thirst protects us, and helps develop a lifetime pattern of finding: *Jesus Saves Me*, the Knowing My God series (ISBN 9780985409029) and *Mud Puddle Hunting Day* (ISBN 9780985409005).

LEARN

PRAISE

Question

Blessed By Curiosity

Questioning is the ability we have to spur and guide our life's growth. The hunger to know is a hallmark practice of earnest discipleship under Jesus, and it is indispensable to a developing spiritual life with him: *Jesus Helps Me*, the Knowing My God series (ISBN 9780989794954) and *Close as a Breath* (ISBN 9780985409067).

LEARN

ABSORB

Persevere

A Season for All

In God's design, "there is a time for everything and a season for every activity under the heavens." As you persevere, he works in your life in unmistakable ways, to achieve your purpose in peace with Jesus: *Jesus Invites Me*, the Knowing My God series (ISBN: 9780985409012) and *Little Seed: A Life* (ISBN: 9780985409074).

LEARN

PRAISE

Early Childhood Books With Newborn Promise

What's so great about board books? Everything going on inside! Small, sturdy board books pack a lot of punch with their beautiful pictures and thoughtfully chosen words. That's why parents love our books and learn from them, too. Reading aloud together becomes a treasured tradition that deepens family ties.

small size for little hands

"My command is this: Love each other as I have loved you."

A sample spread from:
Jesus Shows Me, Knowing My God Series

DISCUSS full page, color photos that delight, inspire, teach

SHARE a passage from Jesus

CONNECT Scripture to life

sturdy pages built to last

My strength helps me win the race, seek the truth, and reach the base.

A sample spread from:
All of Me That You Can't See

UNDERSTAND the importance of a strong spiritual life

APPLY the principles to real-life situations

colorful vibrant artwork

In time, the cold snow changed into warm rain.

It was spring. Little Seed waited.

A sample spread from:
Little Seed: A Life

EXPERIENCE the beauty of nature and growth

LEARN facts about science

Early Childhood Books
With Newborn Promise

"The artwork is amazing, the words are biblical, and the conversations that these books spur are a huge help to parents. So, Learn, Absorb & Praise—true for kids and parents."

—Brad Thomas, Lead Pastor, Austin Ridge Bible Church, Austin, TX

Newborn Promise Parent Tips
Extend your family's experience with the Learn, Absorb & Praise™ board book collection to practice the presence of God in daily life. These simple ideas connect themes from the board books with the Newborn Promise Project, reinforcing a parent's own spiritual growth, too. Available as a free download.